The Secrets of
SUCCESSFUL
LOW-BUDGET
ADVERTISING

About the author

Born forty-eight years ago in the East End of London, Patrick Quinn originally trained as a compositor. But National Service brought him into fortunate contact with the Forces Broadcasting Service in North Africa — for whom he compiled and presented record programmes.

Back in civvy street, he was soon scripting radio plays and writing what he describes as excruciating detective novels.

Armed with all of this published (and unpublished) material, he 'won' his way into a copywriting job with a Bond Street advertising agency. This was largely accomplished by studiously losing to the copy chief in a game of poker dice.

Twenty-five years on, via agencies in Dublin, the USA and Scotland, he has won for his clients just about every advertising award worth winning — including a Grand Prix at the Cork International Film Festival.

The holder of a Private Pilots Licence, and a keen flyer, his remaining ambition is to inherit a brewery.

Books in the series

The Secrets of
SUCCESSFUL
LOW-BUDGET
ADVERTISING

Patrick Quinn

Heinemann Professional Publishing

For the 1st Viscount Horatio Nelson's most ardent admirer

Heinemann Professional Publishing Ltd
22 Bedford Square, London WC1B 3HH

LONDON   MELBOURNE   AUCKLAND

First published 1987
First published as a paperback edition 1988

British Library Cataloguing in Publication Data
Quinn, Patrick
The secrets of successful low-budget
advertising
1. Advertising — Great Britain   2. Small
business — Great Britain
I. Title
659.1'0941   HF5823

ISBN 0 434 91612 9 cased
0 434 91614 5 paper

Photoset by Deltatype Ellesmere Port
Printed by Billing & Sons Ltd
Worcestershire

Contents

Foreword

When I first started out in business for myself in 1964, I ran a small, some might call it minute, tyres and car accessory supply workshop in an Edinburgh back street. Our advertising budget was equally small; but I arrived at the decision early on that I would make every penny count and, wherever possible, make every penny do more than a pennyworth of work.

In this respect, everything you've heard about the Scots being careful with their money – I prefer to call it prudent – was absolutely true. It remains true, as far as I am concerned, to this very day. And right now I spend almost £7 million a year on advertising.

But back to that diminutive tyres and accessories shop. Although there was very little money to spread around on promotions, I knew as certainly as I've ever known anything that, properly advertised, my product was a winner. In essence, I was doing something that had been done for many years. Though not, I am proud to say, with anything approaching my intense conviction, nor with my unique marketing strategy.

The overall idea was three-tiered. First, to provide quality products at a price everyone could afford. This, of course, required judicious pricing and a far lower profit margin; but I was looking for something quite rare in the replacement tyre business – I was looking for volume sales. It was clear to me that volume sales would fully justify the pricing policy. Second, to supply and fit these products with a speed that nobody else could match. Third, to do all this in easily accessible locations.

At the time, if a motorist needed a complete set of tyres,

he would take his car into an ordinary garage . . . and leave it there. Quite often, he would be denied use of the vehicle for an entire day.

This seemed to me not only unnecessary, but also displayed a shocking lack of regard for the customer – the man who was paying for the privilege of having his car taken off the road. Service like this was no service at all; and as unsophisticated as garage equipment may have been in those days, the fitting of five tyres could easily be accomplished by the average mechanic in an hour or so.

Then why was it taking so long? More pertinently, why were garages *allowing* it to take so long? And why had nobody seen fit to do something about it?

The rest, I suppose, is history. I saw the gap in the market and I filled it. I made the principle of top-quality, low-cost products and a 'drive-in' service the norm rather than the exception.

I established the need and I met it. Unequivocally.

Fortunately, this need didn't stop at tyres. It went rapidly on to exhausts, shock absorbers, batteries and radiators. So much so, my company has grown to an impressive 318 outlets and an annual turnover of almost £84 million.

It's true to say that every large business you may care to name began as a single idea. But in order to get any idea off the ground, no matter how revolutionary it might be, you must have a sound marketing policy to back it, and a clear-cut advertising platform from which to launch it.

In this book, Pat Quinn tells you exactly how to formulate both. He proves – and pretty conclusively, too – that anybody with a sound idea for a product or service can make it into the top echelon if they follow the fundamental rules. What he also says (and this really appeals) is that in your promotional scheme of things it's not how much you've got, but what you do with it that counts.

He shows you what to do with it, in no uncertain terms.

He demonstrates that marketing is not, decidedly not, the exclusive domain of the multi-nationals; and he confirms what I have always believed. That effective advertising can be produced by anyone with a small budget on the one hand, and a complex about good advertising on the other.

If you'll take my tip, you will give this book the attention it deserves. To coin a phrase: you can't get better!

Me? Oh, I'm Tom Farmer. You may have heard of my company. It's called Kwik-Fit.

Tom Farmer

Acknowledgements

I am indebted to so many people for their assistance in writing this book that they cannot, I'm sorry to say, all be mentioned by name.

There are, however, a number to whom I must express personal appreciation – otherwise I shall never hear the last of it.

First, to Doug Fox, who took the initial idea for the book virtually on trust. Which just goes to prove what an excellent judge he is.

To Gerry Farrell and Philip Ray, for insisting on having their ideas represented . . . or else.

To Alan Melville, who was gentleman enough to monitor the PR and marketing sections.

And to Tom Farmer, for thinking enough of it to take the trouble to write the Foreword.

Finally, my thanks to Marion and Celia; and only they will ever know for what. And to George Richmond, who lowered his artistic tone in order to produce the 'visuals' for the promotions sections.

Introduction

As a marketing aid, advertising is probably the most effective tool in the entire bag of tricks. And while I take it that you really don't need me to spell out the benefits a company can reap from a sound advertising policy, I will take it that you may need a little help formulating that policy.

That's the purpose of this book.

In effect, it's for low-budget 'advertising managers' of all types, sexes, persuasions and interests. For the man or woman charged, by design or out of necessity, with overseeing the company's advertising effort. He or she will almost certainly be a recruit from the sales or production staff, perhaps even a managing director with nobody on the payroll 'underworked' enough to whom to delegate the job.

(So as not to drive everyone demented in this man/woman, he/she gender allocation briar-patch, may I ask your permission to use the male gender throughout? This is purely for clarity's sake. Please accept my word that for my money, women are as bright and as capable as men ever knew how to be. And, quite frequently, much more so.)

Anyway, this book is for those who have less than massive appropriations to throw around on advertising. It's for retailers; hoteliers; small industrial concerns; garage proprietors; engineering outfits; direct-mail houses; builders, and so on. People who know their own businesses backwards, but who are not achieving the results they expect from their advertising. People who have a sound idea for a new product or service, but who, lacking a marketing or advertising background, have no clear idea of

I

how to launch and promote it. And it's for those who are reluctant, or financially unable, to approach a professional advertising agency – since most agencies are disinclined to handle an account which spends less than £20,000 a year. Indeed, many won't touch you under £50,000; and the bigger boys laugh at anything less that £250,000.

By and large, advertising agencies don't want to know you until you have achieved a certain level of success. Until you have laid all the marketing groundwork and your business is flowing along nicely. When you think about it, this is a sensible enough precaution; because otherwise the agency itself would be shelling out more on servicing the account than it was actually being paid. So I do not argue with the logic of it, only the principle. In this respect then, agencies are very much like banks. They lend you an umbrella when the sun shines, but want it back again as soon as it starts raining.

But let's get back to cases. In the following pages, I shall demonstrate:

(a) How you can prepare your own advertising campaigns; and how to go about recruiting cost-effective professional freelance assistance where necessary.

(b) That a grounding in press, radio and television production techniques will be more than useful when negotiating space and air-time costs.

(c) The basic principles of marketing and how to establish a market for your products and services. 'There may be a gap in the market; but is there a market in the gap?'

(d) How you can launch inexpensive public relations exercises and build a credit balance of goodwill with your various publics.

(e) How to devise and launch 'in-store' promotions and consumer competitions.

(f) The fundamentals of preparing artwork for press advertising, along with the secrets of penning mailshots and leaflets that will be seen, read and acted upon.

In addition, you will find an umbrella package of ready-made, in-store promotions and consumer competitions. As well as full-supporting advertising and PR material. All of which can be adapted and adopted – no matter what your business or your product – straight from the book.

Before we go one whit farther, however, I have a confession to make. With the possible exception of Jack of the famous beanstalk who, if you remember, sold his entire livestock holding for a bag of beans, I am almost certainly the worst businessman you are ever likely to meet. Things like sales forecasts and profit projections are, and will probably remain, a major mystery to me. Unquestionably, I have helped my clients to earn countless millions over the years; and in the so-doing, I have myself made a modest living. Even so, I continue to be underwhelmed by trading accounts, day books and such like ham-stringing paraphernalia.

So if you are hoping to pick up a few tips on business procedure, I'm afraid you've come to the wrong place. But if you want to know how to present your products or services to an audience with money in its pocket, read on. If you want to know how to devise ways of persuading people to shell out in order to own whatever it is you are offering, keep going. And if you feel, as I do, that the word profit is the most agreeable noun in the dictionary, then we have an understanding.

Shall we broaden it?

★　　★　　★

If the advertising business as an unlikely whole (and I include everyone, amateur, or professional, who ever booked space, penned an ad, devised a promotion, laid Letraset, or simply paid someone good money to push their products or services via a given medium), had a signature tune, it might well be that old standard *S'Wonderful*. Because everything in the garden is painted as being flawless and idyllic.

That which isn't miraculous is likely to be fabulous; that which isn't superb is likely to be thrilling or glorious. In fact, it might be fairly said that advertising's approach to the selling of virtually any given product is a load of hyperbolics.

Thus, all male models who aren't hintingly and fruitily gay, are either young, virile and improbably handsome or elderly, distinguished and more I-bought-the-company than even Mr Victor Khyam ever knew how to be. They are not such people as one would normally meet in a day's march, or even a day's jog.

Thus, all female models are, with few exceptions, either bouncy, leggy and disturbingly nubile, or cool, withdrawn, impeccable and just plain disturbing. They, too, are not the kind of people one normally meets in a day's outing.

And more's the pity, I say.

The trouble with them, of course, is that they are too good to be true. They are basically unbelievable; and so are the ads of which they form so monotonous a part.

In the same incredible vein, women are asked to believe that wearing a particular make-up will result in their being swept off by someone approximating the young, virile, etcetera mentioned above driving a souped-up and expensive foreign car. Men, similarly, are invited to swallow the concept that a particular brand of razor will bring them markedly more than their fair share of anything that happens to be going at the time, causing the ladies to flock around them with the insistence of kids around the Pied Piper.

A hair-spray will bring romance; a petrol will bring psychological fulfilment; an anti-acid tablet will make us expert snooker players; a paint will turn our otherwise sensible wives into wide-eyed, adoring morons; and a certain semi-alcoholic beverage will allow us to play chess while up to our armpits in sea-water.

A little of this sort of thing would be fair enough. But a little of it – to coin a phrase – goes a long way; and a lot of it goes too far.

The result of this continual and frenzied excess of excess is that the general public discounts a good 90 per cent of what it reads in advertisements, or hears and sees in commercials.

So here's the point.

It's all very well for advertisers to attempt to preach their indispensability to a mass-production economy and a free enterprise society. Such assertions, true though they may be, cut remarkably little ice with the ordinary, but not so simple man and woman in the street who think of you as, at best, a bunch of over-indulgent clowns and, at worst, a gang of con-artists.

There are, however a few (and happily a growing few) advertisers who are swimming against the general tide and producing advertising which is adult without being pompous, interesting without relying on gimmickry to lend it a spurious liveliness . . . and advertising which is, above all, *believable*.

I shall be saying a lot about believability as we progress. Believe me, it's important.

★   ★   ★

You may be wondering exactly what gives me the divine right to tell you anything about anything. So let's clear a few decks.

During my twenty-five or so years in the advertising business, both as a creative director with ad agencies and as a freelance copywriter, I have won for my respective principals and clients a good measure of profitable business. Not to mention just about every advertising award worth winning – plus a few that aren't.

From this it could be argued that I have learned enough over the years to know roughly what I'm talking about. That's what I'm arguing, anyway; and with any luck, the proof will be in the reading.

It could, of course, turn out that you do not agree with everything I have to say. Come to think of it, you may not agree with any of it. My only defence, should I need one, is that this book is the sum of my own experience in advertising. A distillation of the successes . . . and the failures. And since the formulation of advertising is possibly the most contentious pastime the human mind has ever devised, the opinions I express herein are mine and mine alone

In colourful black-and-white.

Patrick Quinn

1 Advertising – exploring the abstract

What I shall be at pains not to do in this book is present advertising as some kind of simple science and then turn right around and baffle you with it. Advertising is not, and is never likely to be, such a commodity as can be mathematically calculated or computer programmed in order to produce the response you want from it. The creation of advertising is, by and large, a pretty hit and miss business and a matter of doing what your intuition tells you to be right. As I have written in *The Secrets of Successful Copywriting*, advertising cannot be produced on the basis of a set of rules.

I realize that a number of people hold the opposite view and will, at the drop of a hat, present something resembling a cogent argument. I am aware, too, that there are those who earnestly maintain that advertising can be created to a formula. But I know, also, when their efforts are analysed in the cold light of reality, that their success rate is no better (but mostly worse) than the success rate of the non-believers. Meaning those of us who, in our ignorance, reckon advertising to be a calculated gamble usually taken on the strength of creative hunches induced by hard-won experience.

Having said that, there are certain basic principles which must be taken on board – and I shall do my best to communicate them to you. But if it is of any comfort to you, which it should be, I can tell you that the giants of advertising are no more certain that what they are doing is right than you are or I am. The giants are staffed by normal human beings and are subject to the same uncertainties and error that all flesh is heir to. But the giants know those basic principles. They are finger-crossing certain that the material they produce will have a positive effect rather than a negative one. Will do the job it is being paid to do.

Anyway, let's first explore the most fundamental of these principles. I'll call it influence.

Show me a person who is not influenced by advertising and I'll show you someone who lives in a deep cave halfway up the Himalayas. Not to put too fine a point on it, everybody is influenced by advertising in one way or another. These days, it is virtually impossible to remain deaf to its urgings and blind to its caperings. The emphasis, however, should be very firmly placed on 'one way or another'; and I shall return to that in a nonce.

In spite of what you may think, there is nothing new or modern-day about advertising's influence. As far back as the 1700s, the great Dr Johnson was writing: 'Advertisements are now so numerous that they are very negligently pursued; and it has therefore become necessary to gain attention by magnificence of promise and by eloquence . . .'. Which also leads me to suppose that resistance to advertising isn't new either.

Without doubt, the great bulk of advertising does exactly what its originators intend, i.e. to convince an audience that it would be a collective mug not to invest in what is being offered. Even so, a depressing proportion of advertising seems to go right out of its way to alienate its audience, either by insulting its intelligence, by blinding it with bull, or by boring it to distraction – or, in severe cases, a combination of all three. But this is, generally speaking, the accidental result rather than the express intention; and it arises from a general lack of understanding of the principles mentioned. While I hold that nobody can accurately predict the end result – the response they are likely to get – in relation to any advertising they choose to run, there is such a thing as insurance against perpetrating the witlessnesses mentioned above.

It is true to say that the general public makes up its mind pretty rapidly about topics like politics, personalities, sporting events – even commercial enterprises – on the strength of what is fed to it via the various media. It is also true to say that these views and opinions, whether antagonistic or partisan, are largely formed by the manner in which the information is presented. The BBC aside, there isn't a news medium in the UK that can, hand on heart, claim total impartiality on all matters.

From this, then, it can be reasoned with a fair degree of accuracy that *presentation* is the single most important element for successfully getting a message across and making it stick. Anyone with a message to deliver, therefore, would do well to go right out of his way to present it in the clearest, crispest, most concise manner he can devise, so as to draw the maximum positive opinion.

Advertising is no different. It's all about delivering messages. All about winning a favourable response from a market. But advertising, if it is to succeed in its purpose, must be that much more attractive, that much more acceptable, and that much more immediate than any other type of verbal or visual communication.

Let me say here and now that you cannot please all of the people all of the time; and you would be foolish to try, since any advertising produced on this basis would be so bland as to be totally useless. But you will have seen, as I have seen, some perfectly awful advertising. Gross, gauche, puerile, pathetic – we may differ on exactly how, what and why, but it is material that is either so embarrassing or so grating that we wouldn't buy the respective products if we were being paid to do so.

In all of the foregoing respects, then, whether advertising is good or bad, it will have some kind of effect. So in these terms, everybody is influenced by advertising at some time or another, and in one way or another.

And the response you get depends wholly and solely on the presentation you give.

In the course of my work, I am compelled from time to time to read industrial and technical magazines of the engineering genre. It's a chore I wouldn't wish on my worst enemy, or my best competitor – which, in this case, happens to be one and the same, but that's purely by the way. As I leaf through these publications, I am struck by a massive anomaly. The greater proportion of the advertisements are for companies offering components which, we are told, are manufactured to tolerances so precise that, by comparison, the legendary 'fag-paper' takes on the proportions of a sheet of chipboard. Yet as scrupulously exact as their products may very well be, 70 per cent of the ads for these companies are a shambles. In a word, they are sloppy.

Now I am prepared to believe (or at least not to argue with) the proposition that, as manufacturers of fine tolerance bits and pieces, the firms in question are tops. But as advertisers they are not nearly so hot. The headlines are tortuous. The body copy is hyperbole very well carried out. And the pictures – in the unlikely event that they deign to show the product – are unimaginative, flat and usually out of all proportion to the rest of the ad.

This, to me, is just plain daft. Surely the ad managers (or whoever it is in these firms) responsible for countenancing such material are aware that the damage they are doing to the image of their products is such that *no* advertising would be more advantageous.

Why do they do it? They do it because advertising is something which is expected of them and, as far as it goes, plays little part in their overall marketing strategy.

'Look, we only spend twenty-five grand a year on ads,' they burble. 'We do it because our competitors do it. And, to be frank, it doesn't bring us any business to speak of.'

Well of course it doesn't. And it never will the way they do it.

I once convinced a small provincial manufacturer of a range of industrial valves and pipes that if he gave me a free hand with his ads, I would produce an enquiry response comparable to that which his three-man sales team was currently achieving. In the event, I did much better. So, well, in fact, that he immediately doubled his advertising budget and went out and hired an ad agency believing, in his wisdom, that he was now altogether too big to be handled by a lowly freelance.

In truth, all I had done to help get him to that position was tell exactly the same product story as he had been telling for years. The sales-making difference was in the presentation – in the look, the sound and the feel of the ads.

Allow me to give you a pertinent analogy.

Assuming that you could back the claim, you might run an ad which promised to exchange new lamps for old. You might also be in a position to say that inside each and every one of these was a real-life, wish-granting genie. However, if that ad lacks eye-appeal and has no visual strength, be not surprised if you fail to get many takers. Conversely, given that the ad is impeccably designed but neglects in the substance of the words or pictures to put your message across in a believable way, the end result will be the same. You will be stuck not only with a heap of rusting lamps, but also with a host of unemployed genies who are very likely eating you out of house and home.

It's a curious truth in so far as the smaller business is concerned, that even the most spectacular of bargain offers, unless backed by respectable-looking advertising, are doomed to failure. I'll go a step farther and say that the more admirable the offer, the more worthy must be the publicity for it – simply because in being exceptional it incurs an element of doubt. All out-of-the-ordinary offers from small organizations are treated by the market to the 'There must be something wrong with it at that price,' test. 'They are only a little firm, there has to be a catch.'

If you need even more evidence, let me point you in the direction of a national daily newspaper which, many years ago, tried to give away ten-shilling notes. As an investigation into the 'something for nothing' syndrome, they paraded a scruffily-dressed sandwichboard man around Trafalgar Square. His task was to hand out the ten-bob notes to anyone who asked for them. On the face of it, there was no good reason why everyone in sight shouldn't have approached him with outstretched hands, since his sandwichboards proclaimed in no uncertain terms: *Free 10/- Notes*.

Oddly enough, after several hours in the square, he had very few takers. Had that newspaper performed the same exercise a little more respectably, perhaps with a suitably decorated vehicle and a banner or two announcing the name of the newspaper, the chances are that they would have run out of cash in pretty short order.

But, not being mugs, they knew the presentation rule, too!

In the hope that what I've said has gone right home – and that you will never run advertising which doesn't compare more than favourably with the standards I shall set in this book – let's move on and discuss the reasons why you should want, or need, to advertise in the first place.

★   ★   ★

Advertising has a bad name. We of the advertising world are often accused of out-and-out charlatanry, of being cunningly concerned with creating a demand for unwanted products. In the first place it isn't true; and even if it were true it would be entirely defensible in the context of the kind of free, competitive system which most of us prefer, which has provided us with an enviable standard of living and which, if fewer people would monkey around with its workings, would provide us with a higher standard still.

Advertising does not create desires, desires create advertising. If any given product does not meet some *existing* desire or need of the consumer, the advertising for it must immediately fail.

On purely economic grounds, every business needs some kind of publicity. How else can the buying public get to know about it?

But there is more to it than that. A great deal more. Advertising, when it is imaginatively written and inventively designed, should generate for a given company – especially a newly-formed company – an image of substance, dependability and honesty. In essence, here today and here tomorrow, too.

As a manufacturer, or a provider of a service, you may well be as straight as a die and as honest as the day is long. You may also be unswervingly sincere about the merits of your products or services – though if you aren't, what are you doing trying to sell them? Even so, if your advertising omits to project that attitude in a genuine way, you are working with a handicap you neither want nor deserve.

So advertising is more than a device for offering commodities for sale. It is also a vehicle for assuaging any doubts your potential customers may have about doing business with you.

To prove the point, consider if you will the enormous sums of money spent on what is called 'prestige' advertising. This stuff is generally put out by the larger companies of the likes of Shell, Esso and ICI – and it sells nothing except a philosophy. 'We are wonderful people,' is what it says. 'And just look at what we're doing for Britain.' All of which is calculated to give you a nice warm feeling about the company, along with the subconsciously implanted notion that they are good people to deal with.

In all common sense, no small business can afford to get into this league, and neither does it have to, since the nice warm feeling can be made inherent in the advertising it runs day-to-day to promote products and services. How? By talking to people as one human being to another. By cutting out meaningless jargon. By being a little more open than your competitors.

You'll see what I mean later. Right now, it's time we put down some hard and fast reasons for advertising.

1   To create awareness of who you are and what you have to offer.
2   To increase 'traffic' through your shop or showroom. Or produce enquiries that will help increase sales.
3   To encourage market confidence in your products or services.
4   To help compile direct-mail and reps' follow-up lists via coupon response.
5   To counter and, with any luck, upstage competitors' efforts.

All fairly straightforward. Yet eight out of ten small businesses make no attempt to build any of the sentiments behind these objectives into their advertising – presumably hoping that just being on the page is all that is required.

It isn't – not by me it isn't; and neither will it be by your potential customers. So it shouldn't be by you either.

It is not enough to simply list one's wares. It is not enough to invent a better mousetrap, run an ad about it, and hope that people will change their mousetrap-buying habits on your say so. There has to be a secret ingredient. It's called consumer confidence.

Ask any decent salesman what he considers the single most important component of making a sale, and he will very probably tell you that it is the act of gaining the customer's confidence. Once he does that, once he proves that he is neither a con man nor a charlatan of some kind, but is someone who has respect for himself and esteem for whatever it is he is selling, the sale is close to a foregone conclusion.

That very same consumer confidence has to be won via your advertising, if it is to work at all.

Thus far, we have talked briefly around the somewhat nebulous matters of influence, presentation, honesty and confidence. And they are not, decidedly not, such matters as you could pin down and dissect under a microscope. Nevertheless, they exist; and you ignore them at your own considerable risk. I hope to pull them all together in later chapters.

★   ★   ★

All advertising is determined and governed by the amount of money available for spending on it.

How much should that budget be? In the early days of mounting a new business, or launching a new product, 2.5 per cent of your net annual income will not be too much. The idea being that once you are established in the marketplace, you can afford to reappraise things. That doesn't mean to say that the *amount* should be reduced, only the percentage. Because when the business takes off and profits start rolling in, the last thing you should do is stop advertising. Given that you can satisfy the increasing demand, there is no earthly reason not to continue.

For an established business, around 10 per cent of net income is a good budget guideline – though this will depend greatly on the type of business you are in. A retail enterprise with a rapid turnover of a wide range of goods will require to be seen considerably more often in the marketplace than, say, a manufacturing outfit with a smaller market and a limited product range. This is self-evident; but other, less black-and-white situations exist and these should be carefully researched before any money is spent.

I know that some marketing people will say that basing an advertising budget on a percentage of sales is illogical, since sales are more likely to be influenced by advertising rather than vice versa. But you have to start somewhere – right?

There is a further point worth mentioning here. When times are bad, when the cold economic climate begins to grip, many a businessman starts looking around for ways of making expenditure cuts. He cuts back on staff; he cuts back on telephone and postage usage; he cuts back on company vehicles; and he cuts back on advertising.

Oh, brother!

While it is all very right and proper to reduce the expenditure in most of the above areas, to cut back on advertising in such circumstances is plain, straightforward short-sightedness.

Let's get our drinks straight. The time to make a big publicity splash is when things are bad. The time to show the world how well we are doing is when we are not doing well at all. That way, we will be sure of getting more than our fair share of the market – albeit a limited one. That way we will have cash flow and turnover. And that way we shall stay in business until the good times come rolling round again. The lion's share of a very modest cake is a sight better than no cake at all.

One of the cleverest advertising men I have ever met once put this into succinct perspective. 'In every business,' he said, 'there is appearance . . . and there is reality. Keeping your head just above the waterline is the reality. Being seen to be successful – however little basis that has in fact – is the appearance.'

There are any number of precedents to demonstrate the validity of being seen to be on top. But one example should suffice. Several years ago, during one of our many freezes, a large and highly-regarded manufacturer of non-alcoholic beverages (whom I shall refrain from naming to save them any embarrassment) saw that sales of one of its products had dropped dramatically. This drop levelled out at a point where turnover only just matched production, distribution and marketing costs.

After much deliberation, the company cut its £250,000 advertising budget for this particular brand completely in half, reasoning that the £125,000 thus saved would represent a profit and might at least keep the shareholders at bay for a while.

What happened? Predictably, over a period of only a few months, sales dropped straight through the basement floor. Things had never been worse; and redundancy notices started flying in all directions. Then, out of the blue, a quite bright spark hit upon the idea of reinstating the advertising budget to the full and original £250,000. In the event, however, the company calculated that to get back to the earlier, disappointing sales levels, it would need to double the amount, i.e. increase the spend to £500,000.

Until sales took off again, at the coming of a defrosted climate, that particular brand was losing a quarter of a million pounds a year.

To sum all of this up, I would say that just like life, you only get out of advertising what you put into it. In many ways, the amount you spend will determine the volume of response you get – since more money spent means more advertising bought and, with any luck, a wider audience reached or a higher volume of readings of your particular material gained. But this is not wholly true in every respect. I contend, and quite confidently as it happens, that one cleverly written ad is better – ten times better – than ten ill-conceived ones. The reason is this. One good ad will have ten times more in-built memorability.

Memorability is another of those recondite characteristics which, along with influence, presentation, etc., should be endemic in every ad you produce. More than that, memorability is the sum total of all the other features. And memorability, when it is all boiled down, is the quality you are striving for.

But back to percentages.

I said earlier that around 10 per cent of net income is a not unreasonable figure to spend on advertising. I would qualify that by saying that there is no value in adhering to a set percentage if results aren't up to expectations. In this unhappy circumstance – when you know for certain that your ads are not working, not producing enquiries – there are several points to consider:

1   You are not spending enough to properly reach the market in any significant way.
2   What you are spending is missing – is going over the heads of, or is being rejected by – your target audience.
3   Your advertising needs reappraising and overhauling.
4   A combination of all three.

One of the greatest wastes of money is to run advertising without linking it to your total marketing plan. Thus, an advertising gambit which declines to match the marketing strategy is worse than useless. For instance, assume for a moment that you are in the retail stair-carpet business and you advertise on a regular basis in the local press. What a chump you would be to go into a freesheet newspaper whose distribution area is predominently made up of high-rise flats, bungalows and bedsitters.

Don't laugh – I have witnessed worse. Marketing faux pas of this execrable sort are constantly made.

How about this for a classic?

During the Second World War, British Intelligence decided to stir up a modicum of discontent among the troops in the German front line. Consequently, it air-dropped leaflets on the German positions. These leaflets, in German, told in extremely lurid terms what the handsome blonde giants of the SS were up to at home with the fraus and fräuleins of the men doing the fighting. What with the Nazi philosophy of strength through joy and Hitler's express intention of breeding an Aryan race, the leaflets found a ready, if slightly uneasy audience. After a while, copies of the leaflets fell into the hands of the German High Command which, beside itself with fury, produced its own leaflets refuting the entire sordid business.

So far, so good. But then it made two unredeemable errors. First, it produced the leaflets in English. Second, it dropped them on the British lines. The tommies, as you may imagine, were suitably perplexed – having, of course, no knowledge of the initial 'mailing'; and the Germans, well, they just went on worrying about the domestic scene.

Which just goes to show how important it is, before undertaking advertising, to define your target market with care – and to approach it with accuracy.

★   ★   ★

And that brings me neatly on to the problems of determining the market and how to reach it.

Manifestly, before you book so much as one centimetre of space, you must resolve these two critical questions. What is the market for your product or service? And where do you locate that market?

It goes without saying, I assume, that where you make your promotional gambit is just as important as how you make it. You may also go along with me that prior to establishing how, you should substantiate in no uncertain terms exactly *who* it is you want to reach.

In Chapter 4, I will lay down some guidelines for doing just that. In the meantime, let's examine the types of media available.

Press
National and local newspapers. Freesheets. Business trade and technical magazines. Local community and club and association publications.

Radio and TV
There are fifty-nine commercial radio stations and seventeen independent television companies, including satellite TV. These can be employed on a local or national basis.

Mailers
Categories are simple sales letters reproduced on company letterheads, or specially printed folders. In the latter case, the opportunities for inventive and creative presentations are virtually limitless. Mailers are sent via the normal postal-delivery system.

Door-to-door leaflets
Otherwise known as knock-and-drop leaflets. These are usually single-sheet productions which are delivered either by specialist companies, by the company's own staff, or by arrangement with the GPO. (Obviously, PO-delivered knock-and-drops are distributed only to those households in a given area to which the postman is calling on that particular day. Thus, only a fraction of homes in an area will be contacted.)

Transport and poster advertising
This covers most public service vehicles – including some taxis. It embraces bus interiors and exteriors, subway train interiors, and poster space at bus termini and railway stations.

So there you have a general background to the abstract features of advertising. We should now move on to the meatier, more tangible principles.

The constituent parts of a press ad
The following is the textbook definition (more or less) of what a perfectly conceived ad should consist of. I include it, not to ram formula down your throat, but to present a yardstick by which to work. Equally, I'm not saying that every ad should contain all of these ingredients. My object is merely to furnish an outline for those who have never considered the mechanics of an advertisement.

The headline
A strong statement which features the major selling point of the product. (It's cheaper, faster, operates more efficiently, and so on.) This is the unique selling proposition.

The illustration
Not mandatory by any means, but it should, in any case, visually reinforce the claim made in the headline. It may do this by demonstration of how the product works; how it is constructed; or how much smaller/larger it is compared with other products.

Figure 1   *The constituent parts of a press ad*

The body copy

1 Should open with a lead paragraph enlarging upon the headline. (How much cheaper, faster, more efficient, etc.)

2 A series of facts in support of that benefit claim. (It's cheaper because of a new production technique; it's faster because of improved design/engineering.)

3 A short dissertation on any peripheral benefits. (It comes in a choice of colours/materials/sizes.)

4 A caution to the reader that he will miss a good opportunity if he fails to buy the product. (It's a limited duration offer; he won't be operating as efficiently without the product; or he will lose money/status without it.)

5 An enjoiner to find out more, or to go out and buy the product – with details of how and where. (Take a test-drive, see a demonstration, drop in, phone for the facts.)

6 A pay-off line relating back to the benefit in the headline.

The logotype

A visual device for linking the advertiser to the product, or range of products, in his corporate scheme of things. Its purpose is to help the market identify the source wherever and whenever seen.

The tag-line

A short statement summing up the product or the trading philosophy of the company. (*We take good care of you.*)

The name, address and telephone number of the advertiser

That's roughly what the book says; and you can take it or leave it.

Were I you, while I shouldn't reject it out of hand, I should most definitely not attach to it the authority of the law of the Medes and Persians. You won't – will you?

2   Advertising – the nuts and bolts

The financial limitations placed upon the small business advertiser will render it almost certain that, in the early stages of operation, he or she will be restricted to the use of press advertising as a means of approaching a market. (I use the word press loosely, and include trade and technical journals in the term.) Taking it in the round, the press has much to be said for it. In fact, it has everything to be said for it, since the amount of coverage you can get for the price – not to mention, in the case of specialist journals, the accurate zeroing-in on a given market segment and virtually no wastage – is second to none. I'll rehash that slightly and say that in only one instance does the press come second; and that's to a carefully calculated, recipient-selected and personalized mail-shot. And I don't mean a sales letter. I mean specifically printed literature and/or accompanying samples or executive incentive-gift. On the grounds of cost alone, though (the price of producing the mailing, customer research and postage) these necessitate a strictly limited number of blue-chip targets who are genuinely in the market for your products, and who will be likely to take the bait strongly enough for you to come out of it smelling of roses and covered in financial gain.

So the press is a pretty effective instrument. It's also one which will let you down with a substantial bump should you misuse it or abuse it. If you read the following with the attention it deserves, you will do neither.

At any rate, it is possible – very possible – to make a big impression in the press on the strength of a less than Midasian budget. In this regard, though, every penny must be made to count; and every ad insertion needs to work a damn sight harder than its wealthier competitors.

Which means that your advertising will need to be that much more original in its approach and that much more striking in its appearance. In other words, your stuff should receive considerably more than its fair share of attention.

To reach this happy state of affairs, you will be wise to latch on to one or two important precepts. These may, in the event, strike you as rather obvious, but not so obvious that thousands of advertisers fail to implement them on a regular and anguishing basis.

Allow me to begin like this. There is a television programme on Channel 4 which allows all and sundry to air their respective views on camera. Similarly, after each early evening news broadcast, the same station gives up five minutes of its air time to individuals with particular (and quite often peculiar) axes to grind. Now, the ordinary folk concerned in these sessions take the opportunity in both hands and make their positions plain with no uncertain enthusiasm. All right, given an urgent point of view and a large soapbox from which to broadcast it, you might conclude that nobody but a fool would lose the chance. And all power to them.

So why, I ask myself, do so many advertisers take space in newspapers and magazines and then proceed to say nothing of any consequence? The question is rhetorical, but the sentiments of it are none the less irrefutable. It happens all the time, day in day out.

Someone once said that much of today's advertising is like the man who winks at a girl in the dark. He knows what he's doing, but nobody else does.

What I am saying is that the originators of acres of advertising work one sees betimes seem unable to come to terms with the simple proposition that ads which say nothing of any consequence, are quietly admitting that they have nothing of any consequence to say.

Even worse, and even more stupidly, they are conceding that they have nothing of any consequence to *sell*.

Which enjoins me to frame the first precept.

To create a buying response, to instil a desire to own or at least know more about a product or service, an advertisement should say something of very real interest to the reader. Better still, it should either constitute an offer, or make a readily discernible promise.

And this offer or promise is far more likely to be absorbed if it is evident to the reader at first glance.

You may care to go along with me when I say that in my not so humble opinion the headline is the single most important element of any ad. If you don't care to, then all I can say is you are certainly not alone in your reactionary views, on account of every designer and visualizer I have ever met feels exactly the same way.

Nevertheless, I defy anyone to argue with the well-documented fact that when presented with a new ad a reader will, four times out of five, scan the headline before examining the picture or reading the body copy. If this is indeed the case (though I am as circumspect about statistics as the next person) our headline wins, if not by a knockout, certainly on a fair aggregate of points.

This said, it follows that the aforementioned offer or promise should be contained, writ large, in the headline.

The exceptions to this sweeping generalization are many. Like the ad, for instance, which asks a question apposite to the nature of the product. An ad for a hair-colourants range, say, might contain half-a-dozen, full-colour head-and-shoulders pictures of a young woman – the same young woman in each case – wearing her hair in different colours and different styles. The headline would then maybe say: '*How often have you wished you were someone else?*'

No overt offer, no clear promise. Even so, there's an implied assurance that by using this product the reader, if she so desires, may readily change her appearance.

With ads of this type there can be no falling out. It's the faceless, say-nothing, do-nothing, *suggest* nothing material that I get so hot under the collar about.

But wait, you cry, leafing through your morning paper. Only about 60 per cent of the ads herein make an offer or a promise – or even a veiled suggestion. Why? I'll tell you, I reply. Take a second look and you will discover that the offending 40 per cent either don't need to, because they fall into the prestige category we discussed a while back, or they are what, for want of a better phrase, I shall define as creative enormities perpetrated by people who either don't know any better or don't care to know any better. They are ads written by trainee copywriters who have hit upon an excrutiating pun which, in their credulity, they view as pertinent and which they use in spite of its unfittedness – and almost certainly in the absence of their bosses. They are ads written by ad agency personnel who started out with something noteworthy and germane to the job in hand, but who were edited, expurgated, or just plain overruled by their clients. And they are ads conceived out of blissful ignorance of what I have said above by company sales staff who have, usually against their will, been summarily elevated to publicity duties. (If the latter know what's good for them, they will buy this book forthwith, digest its pearls of wisdom then, in some perfectly bourgeois manner shower me with gifts out of undiluted gratitude).

One of nature's masochists, I have before me at this moment a whole sad wad of current ads. Shining examples of the sort of work I am talking about. Each of them is characteristic in that the headline tells me, a possible customer, nothing of any consequence about the goods which are presumably being offered.

If you have ever looked twice at a stamp . . .	This one's for the philatelic services offered by the Royal Mail.
Focus on fashion	For a mail–order house catalogue.
Sitting pretty	A department store's attempt to sell its fashion department.
Language learning break-through	A postal tuition course.
Jeepers creepers, where'd you get that home	For a construction firm.

Am I being fair? I assure you that in none of these

instances does the supporting illustration (and in one case, not even the body copy) do anything to rescue the line from insignificance or give it any selling quality.

I am not suggesting for one moment that all ads, in order to fit my hypothesis, should present themselves as black and white statements, or as bland descriptions of a product and its price.

Far from it. I am all in favour of ads which titillate, which provide amusing diversion, which stimulate imagination and arouse curiosity. Come to think of it, I have myself written a few much such. What I am setting you against – dead against – is advertising that says nothing.

In the first place, as a small business person you can't afford it; and in the second place, you are far too bright.

It's worth remembering, too, that all advertising, no matter how joyously conceived, has the universally despised stigmata of bare-faced commercialism. To put it another way, nobody but the originators care very much whether it exists or not. Couple that with the fact that it will be placed cheek-by-jowl with many similar pieces of work, each screaming for attention, and you have a situation fraught with uncertainty.

Realizing this, you should go right out of your way to ensure that your advertising is that much more compelling than anything in the immediate vicinity of the reader.

To draw our thoughts on headlines together, perhaps I should offer a final for instance.

It's a genuine, but vastly inappropriate headline for a full-page press ad, written some time ago by the publicity wallah of a substantial provincial garage. This outfit had taken half-a-dozen models of a middle-of-the-range production-line car and given them the executive treatment. They fitted stereo radio and cassette systems, deep-pile carpets, steel exhaust system, sound-proofing, under-sealing, dashes of extra chrome here and there, plush seat covers, and various bells and whistles for the dashboard. (All of which, I suppose, now come as standard on the majority of cars – but at the time it was an innovation.)

Anyway, the car was also resprayed in a tasteful two-tone

black and grey. It was then christened the Executive IV and priced at only £700 more than standard cost, making it about £500 cheaper than the next car up in the range.

It was a Ford in Jags clothing; and a splendid marketing idea aimed directly at the man who wanted a more expensive looking car than he could properly afford.

So much so, it certainly deserved better treatment than it actually got. Here's what it got:

MOTORISTS DON'T KNOW ANY BETTER!

The remainder of the ad consisted of a picture of the car, plus a combination picture of the many extra fittings and bits of gadgetry you could expect to find on it, along with a stick of body copy extolling the vehicle's virtues.

As you can see, the line neither offers nor promises. It even neglects to name the car. Presumably the author thought this unnecessary on the wildly optimistic premise that his faintly amusing headline would do all the pulling that was required.

Lines like this have no meaning and, therefore, no value. For a potential buyer to gain anything from the ad, he or she would be compelled to delve more deeply into it where, with any degree of luck, the product story has been laid out.

Mostly, people won't bother to do that if the headline hasn't grabbed their attention and thereby excited their curiosity enough for them to want to find out more. Nine times out of ten, unless they are in the market for your particular product at that specific moment, they will dismiss the ad out of hand.

And that's fatal. Because an ad – any ad – should not only speak to people who may be customers at that time, but also to those who could well become customers at a later date.

If an advertisement can generate this degree of memorability it is, in effect getting two bites at the cherry. Offhand, I can think of nothing more worthwhile than an ad which has imposed itself so graphically upon the reader's unconscious that it jumps to mind a week or a fortnight after the event.

How much better, then, if our garage friend had given deeper thought to his product, considered his market more shrewdly, and brought the two together as one might introduce a timorous guest to the buffet spread at a party. Something like this:

THE EXECUTIVE IV
EVEN STANDING STILL IT MOVES YOU

How very much better. And were we to include a subhead to the effect of:

(Limited edition: £X,XXX)

we should have the foundations of an ad offering an out-of-the-ordinary car at a reasonable price, along with the inferred promise that its good looks will turn a few heads and give the owner the kudos of an exclusive car.

All right, now let's move on to the second most important element of the ad – the illustration.

★　　★　　★

People, especially ad-designer-type people, never tire of telling me that a picture (photograph, line drawing, wash drawing, scraperboard, air-brush illustration) is worth a thousand words. Were this only true, then we benighted copywriters could all pack up, go home and take up something sensible and generally more rewarding. Like shark-baiting or barbed-wire hurdling.

In any case, the comparison is odious. Any writer of an ad who had it in mind to put down more than 250 words would be well advised not to bother. But that's copy – at the moment we're talking pictures.

There is no doubt in my mind that an ad is greatly assisted in its aims by the inclusion of an illustration. But only so long as it is a relevant pic, an appropriate pic, a pic suited to the job in hand. One that either reinforces or augments the headline.

The disturbing practice of using illustrations that have no bearing on the product story is anathema to me. To be fair, though, these are usually accompanied by headlines which themselves have no bearing on the product story either. They are designed to be eye-catchers or 'stoppers'; yet just as a spectacular road accident will stop passers-by, the interest wanes very quickly once it is seen that the injuries sustained are superficial ones. Metaphorically speaking, one has to spill a lot of blood – or a lot of beans – to hold the attention of someone you have grabbed by the throat and dragged, unwillingly, towards your particular piece of sensationalism. More so, as it happens, than that required when the casual observer is encouraged by a gentle nudge and a knowing wink to investigate what you are all about.

As an advocate, although not a fanatic, of directness in advertising, I see little point in showing a picture of a diamond, adorning it with the headline: 'Flawless', throwing in copy which draws the analogy between the perfectness of diamonds and your product, and hoping that it will sell fitted kitchens.

It almost certainly won't.

Although indirection of this type appears to be intelligent indirection, leading the reader on, like a left-feint laying someone open to a right-cross, it is unrewarded indirection. Because these ads feint without crossing or, in the majority of cases, neither feint nor cross but merely stand there with their fists up.

Ads which draw analogies are, unless the analogy concerned is very closely related to the product being advertised, dangerous. No – dangerous is too strong a word. They are largely a case of frittering away money on something that few people will read and even fewer people will believe.

Then why, you may ask, are they produced with such frequency? Answer: they are easy to do. You can compare anything with anything if you really try. After all, if you looked at the matter closely, I've no doubt that there are things which I have in common with J. S. Bach. But I take leave to doubt that they will form the basis of one of the great sales stories of all time.

Lastly, before we rejoin the subject we are supposed to be talking about – illustration – a couple of minor general pleas.

Will all those manufacturers of boxes, cartons and containers who have been using ads headlined: '*Boxing clever*' kindly give it a rest? It wasn't all that funny in the first place. The same goes for various packaging people who, for year after interminable year, have gone around proclaiming that '*We've got you covered.*' I just thought I'd mention it.

Illustration, then. If I had a pound for every time I have seen a chessboard featured in an ad, I should not be larking around like this giving literature a bad name. Not a bit of it. I should be doing something useful – like testing whisky sours beside a pool in the Bahamas.

The same goes for door-keys, Monopoly boards, acorns and Rubik's cubes. These are just a few, and I mean a few, of the classic clichés of advertising. As, of course, are the lines accompanying them: '*It's your move*', etc. But every day, in every way, budding clichés are born by the use in ads of analogous illustrations and by maltreating the patently obvious with visual puns that would give pause to *Tom and Jerry*.

Some schools of advertising have a very real aversion to showing the product under any circumstances. They tie themselves in knots trying to escape illustrating phosphor-bronze bearings, electronic circuit boards, or commercial ovens. This manifests itself most strongly, as you may judge from the examples I've given, in industrial advert-ising; and it is manifestly unnecessary.

If you are the manufacturer of a range of stainless-steel springs, said springs will no doubt be something in which you take a proper and justifiable pride. Then why should you not depict them in your advertising? What prevents it? The springs are not that attractive? Your customers already know what a stainless-steel spring looks like?

Well, please yourself. But I am here to tell you that a good photographer or illustrator can render the ugliest of items quite inviting. (Indeed, I have a photograph or two of myself to prove the point.)

In many respects, the furnishers of non-tangible products
– insurance, express parcel delivery, travel, tuition, legal
services, and so on – are fortunate in that they are able to go
wherever their creativity takes them, not being hampered,
as it were, by the albatross of cast-iron products.

Notwithstanding that, wandering too far from the
product story can be very counterproductive, indeed.
Most of what I regard as faults in this area come about by a
predilection among some advertisers for jumping onto the
bandwagon of any new fad, fashion or vogue that happens
to be passing.

In a visual context, everything from hula-hoops, through
skateboards, space-invader machines, computer graphics
and BMX bikes has been done; and not only done, but done
in. On the headline writing side, phrases such as 'I've
started so I'll finish' (*Mastermind*), 'Come on down' (*The
Price is Right*) and 'Gizza job' (*Boys from the Black Stuff*) – not
to mention numerous subsequent catch-phrases originating
in programmes that I haven't yet seen, since my TV set is so
old it only picks up repeats – have been dragooned into
advertising's cause.

Nothing wrong with that. Nothing, that is, if you were
among the first half-dozen to use a given line or a given
visual approach. It is when you are among the latter 600 that
the gilt tends to wear off the gingerbread. At which time,
your ads are talking to an audience that is not only already
very familiar with the theme but is, in all probability, up to
here with it.

It wasn't me, but somebody once said that art and
commercialism are not compatable. I find that hard to live
with. I have seen certain illustrations for products that you
drive, walk on, pour down your throat or wear that, if they
are not art, are something very much approaching it. And if
these are not true reflections of the society in which we live,
then neither is the work of Hogarth and his contemporaries
whose illustrations, you will recall, were available for hire
at the time. If that wasn't commercialism, what is?

There is no question that advertising, rather than setting
trends, follows them faithfully. But if, in your advertising,

you can latch on to a vogue in advance of the rest, or even help promote one, you will be quids in.

★   ★   ★

It may be a little late in the day for many of you, but my advice to you is none the less unequivocal. Leave the women alone.

With the possible exception of aerial photographs of your factory, putting pictures of nubile young women into ads is just about the single most destructive thing you can do. To be more specific, what I am warning you against are pictures of nubile young women featured with practically nothing on. What I am dead against is their use in advertisements where they are completely unrelated to the product or service being promoted.

If you are in the bra business, or the bust-developer business or, rather more loosely, in the ladies' fashion business, by all means show what your product looks like, and what it does, in relation to those who may be buying it and using it. In this regard, female models are pretty much essential. But if you happen to be in the drop forged steel roller-bearing business, or the fast-food business, or whatever, the decision to use half-clad women to push your goods is bound to be counterproductive.

In such cases, it seems to me, their employment reflects adversely upon the advertiser. He is saying, in effect, that he can't think of any interesting way to talk about or show what he is trying to sell. It is a dull product with nothing particular to commend it. Therefore he will show as much as he dares of a girl in order to attract old roués like Patrick Quinn.

This, on the face of it, is not an unfair argument. To be sure, such ads *do* catch the eye of unrepentants like me – and the world is full of us. But with what result? There is nothing simpler than getting yourself noticed. If I were to walk down Bond Street wearing nothing but a 'Biggles' flying helmet and wellies, I dare say I would achieve more popular notice than Wham and Lord Lichfield put together.

But where would it get me – apart from the nearest police station?

That sex sells I cannot and will not deny. But sex sells things that are *related* to sex. You may, of course, disagree and say that showing a nude these days, in the face of the feminist lobby, displays a certain amount of nerve and conviction – separates the men from the boys. Even so, don't be surprised if many of your customers arrive at the conclusion that you have separated yourself from your sanity.

I have only once deliberately and knowingly used pulchritude to sell a product that bore no relationship to sex. The product was the service offered by a very large garage in a very large provincial town. This garage boasted a sixteen-pump forecourt which was presided over by a most attractive and exceptionally personable blonde girl. All of her male customers, without exception, were bowled over by her personality and looks.

They knew her, they called her by her first name, and she encouraged their attentions. She was, without doubt, a most proficient seller of petrol and a real asset to her firm.

Thus, with her permission, I wrote a series of radio commercials around her. She wasn't featured, but the gist of these pieces was a conversation between two men who, with good taste and humour, made it clear that they bought more petrol than they needed/visited so-and-so's garage more often than necessary, strictly on account of the magnetism of said blonde.

It worked – and it worked well. And I defend it because the garage made extra profit, and the girl came out of it rather nicely since she picked up a tidy commission on sales.

She was (and still is, I hope) a unique selling proposition in every sense of the phrase.

★   ★   ★

Shall we say a word or two about cartoon illustrations? Oh all right.

Well, I like them. Aside from being great fun to work on, they also have an almost universal appeal.

Alas, I am sad to say that these days cartoons appear to be falling out of favour with advertising people. Although used, as they often are nowadays, in comic-strip form and with story-line which genuinely expects itself to be taken as a serious, 'real-life' situation, their demise may be a not altogether bad thing.

These strips usually run something like this.

Frame 1   *Important client to the senior partner of the Acme Architectural Co.:*
'You've got the job, Mike – but I need twenty sets of the drawings and specifications for our board meeting on Friday.'

Frame 2   *Senior partner to secretary:*
'How on earth can we get all this documentation ready in time, Muriel?'

Frame 3   *Secretary on phone to the Facsimile Copier Co.:*
'I need a copier that will reproduce up to A2 in four colours.'

Frame 4   *Various pictures of a Facsimile copier being installed – against the clock.*

Frame 5   *Client's board meeting with the completed documents in view. Client to senior partner:*
'Congratulations, Mike – a very professional job.'

Frame 6   *Various pictures of the Facsimile copier range, plus contact details.*

They are toe-curlers, are they not. And I suspect that the response they evoke is pretty embarrassing, also.

I cannot make up my mind whether or not we are expected to take these offerings at their face value. Palpably, though, cartoons should be employed for what cartoons do best. To satirize; to bring a situation into comic relief; or to make a set of circumstances much, *much* larger than life.

Which is not what the likes of the above achieve. Faced with the same job, I would set out to produce a single cartoon of, say, Tweedle-Dum and Tweedle-Dee and use their mutual resemblance to point up the Facsimile story.

Agreed, it may not be the best way to do it, but it is, I submit, a more believable way. Old hat? Certainly – on account of I used it years ago.

So what am I saying? Only that by all means enlist cartoons for your advertising, and give all and sundry a smile. But at all costs refrain from making yourself a laughing stock.

People tend not to want to do business with buffoons.

Figure 2   *The four main types of illustration*

(a) Half-tone illustration

The technique of breaking up a photographic image into a series of dots in order to reproduce the full tone range of that photograph. The breaking up is achieved by inserting a screen over the plate as it is exposed.

The density of the dots determines the reproduction quality, i.e. low-density for coarse papers – newsprint, etc.; high-density for good quality art papers, and the like.

A squared-up half-tone 'plate' currently costs around £15 per square 25 mm to make.

Courtesy Cessna Aircraft.

(b) Line drawing

A picture drawn in black-and-white with no screen or tints to enhance it. It can be as simple or as complicated as the artist cares to make it.

Costs vary according to the skill and reputation of the artist. However, the line drawing shown here could be produced for less than £60.

Much line work is derivative. Meaning that many artists use 'references' of existing material on which to base their 'original' drawing. From the low-budget advertiser's point of view this is no bad thing, since it saves a lot of origination time.

Courtesy Tony Haughey.

(c)   Line and tone illustration

A much more sophisticated use of pen and ink. This technique usually involves the laying down of 'mechanical' or proprietory tints (Letraset, for example), plus additional shading with brush, crayon or pen.

A near-photographic effect can be achieved because of the added dimension that the varying tones produce.

Obviously, this process takes longer to make than simple line work and will be proportionally more expensive. You wouldn't get much change from £150 for the line/tone picture reproduced here.

Courtesy Jim Sharp.

(d) Schafline illustration

Schafline is a commercial process whereby ordinary photographic work is given a high-definition 'line conversion' treatment. In the conventional half-tone process, the image is broken down into dots; but with Schafline the image is made up of a diagonal line screen. This gives an extremely crisp, very clean reproduction quality.

Schafline is a hi-tech derivation of the old mezzotint. You can achieve your own mezzotint effect simply by photocopying a 'contrasty' photograph.

From photograph supplied, this Schafline print would cost about £30.

Courtesy Schafline Limited.

3   More nuts and bolts

It is my pleasure, now, to introduce you to copy. Body copy.

The grey squiggles that sit unobtrusively between the headline and the name of the company. The lexicographic jumble sale of hand-me-down superlatives and clichés with which the writer proves to the world at large that you can commit murder and get away with it. The avalanche of facts, figures, dimensions, specifications, weights, materials and qualities very few people notice and even fewer bother to read.

Is any of this true? Do people really dismiss copy so off-handedly? Woefully, it very often is and they do. And I am talking not only about the people who are asked to read it – the people it is aimed at. Some of the most indifferent, and therefore some of the most culpable in this regard, are the people who write it.

But, surely, body copy is put into an ad, or should be put into an ad, so as to be read? So as to communicate a message? So as to create interest? So as to provoke a buying response?

Well, I know that, and now you know it – and I apologize if you already did; yet one can, when one is in a charitable mood, point to the copy in upwards of 40 per cent of all ads in the certain knowledge that there aren't too many of us sharing the same enlightenment. In other words, the copy in four out of ten ads neither communicates, interests, nor provokes – not in our meaning of the word, anyway.

For irrefutable proof, just pick up the nearest newspaper or magazine and see for yourself what a dreary, lifeless, uninspired mess of pottage there is masquerading as advertising copy.

If at this stage in the game, you are uncertain of your ground, unsure that you are as yet qualified to judge – or you may simply subscribe to the view that before you can be a critic, you must first be a performer – allow me to give you a few pointers.

Copy, whether written by an amateur or a professional must, if it is to succeed, embody one essential characteristic: readability. Regardless of its content, it must be clear, crisp and concise. To put it into words of one syllable, put it into words of one syllable. Clarity in copy is not only desirable it is imperative.

The great enemy of clarity in so far as amateur writers are concerned is their inability to present their proposition in a logical form, as a step-to-step progression. From the standpoint of the professional, there are any number of obstacles, the major one of these being the imposition of deadlines.

Allowed minutes rather than hours to dash off a piece of work, the professional will slip into automatic and produce what amounts to verbal wallpaper which, albeit competent, lacks any sign of life or sparkle.

A copywriter acquaintance of mine was once presented by a client with a deadline of a little under thirty minutes to knock out a job that he would, under ideal conditions, have struggled to complete in a day. He begged and he pleaded for more time. 'After all,' he argued, 'I want to do a good job.'

The client remained unmoved. 'I don't want it good,' he said. 'I want it now!'

Readability, aside, the best examples of copy also project sincerity, they make their claims believable to a cynical and indifferent audience. They do this by 'levelling' with the reader; by addressing him or her person-to-person; human being to human being. They present their case rather as one would convince a friend that, if he will lend it, you will return his car/lawnmower/money promptly and in one piece. With frankness and honesty. And they make their pitch in simple terms in simple language.

Copy should be intelligible to even the dimmest of

readers. The structure should be such as to leave no room for doubt and no margin of error. This is why the very best of copy is, on the face of it, so very elementary – so wonderfully uncomplicated. But in its simplicity it is also slick and ingenious. It contains wordplay acceptable to everyone; it uses phrases which delight even the most jaundiced of eyes.

Perhaps I may give you an example of good copy in action. This was written by one of the finest wordsmiths in the business for an ad for the Stanley range of handtools. It's probably unnecessary to give you the headline, but I include it because it happens to be a beauty.

WHY YOUR FIRST STANLEY TOOL IS UNLIKELY TO BE YOUR LAST

Experience has taught us that the man who needs one good tool will sooner or later require another.

This is why we find it pays to maintain a high standard of quality.

A very high standard.

Our Steelmaster hammer, for instance, is just one example of the many thousands of yardsticks we set ourselves.

The carefully balanced head is tempered to be shock-absorbent at the centre.

A tubular steel shaft provides the ideal degree of 'bounce'.

And, to give a firm, non-slip grip, we impregnate the rubber handle with flock.

We apply the same attention to the design of our fibreglass, hickory and ash handled hammers.

Our screwdrivers, saws, chisels, rules, braces, hand drills, planes, knives, levels, bevels and squares. And, of course, our range of building tools.

Whatever Stanley tool you buy, you aren't just buying a reputation.

You're buying what earns that reputation.

Not a word too many. Not a word out of place. This piece of work is clean, unfettered, easily absorbed; and I know for a fact that it, along with other ads in the same series, helped sell more tools than any campaign before it. I'll grant that it may not be the best piece of copy ever written – it may not even be the third best – though if you examine it carefully, you'll see that it fulfils all of the requirements talked about earlier.

Observe how nonchalantly it sets up the proposition that the best of tools are synonymous with Stanley tools without ever saying so. How confidently it puts itself across as an entirely believable promise without offering reams of tortuous argument in justification. How easily it persuades without badgering. And how crystal clear the whole thing is.

As for the pay-off paragraphs, they are exemplary.

To do work of this kind and have any hope of success, the writer must obviously have the backing of a first-class product. And to write soft-sell copy – of which this is a profound example – the product will needs be already well known in the marketplace. Even so, the frame of mind that produces copy of this nature (and it's only a frame of mind) can, with practice, be slipped into at will.

We shall discover exactly how a little later.

So now we know what constitutes good copy – don't we? To make sure we never write any of the fruitless or even harmful stuff, however, we'd better know what it looks like. I therefore propose to define duff, or misconceived copy under three headings – there are more, but three should be sufficient to be getting on with.

The scream and shout

Advertising is undoubtedly the major way in which a company presents itself to the public at large; and what people think of a company determines, for the most part, whether or not they will consider buying from it. It would seem only prudent, therefore, that when approaching perfect strangers, a company should wear a reasonable suit and adopt a reasonable set of manners – and that it should display a reasonable amount of integrity. Thus, its advertising should not consistently shout at people, or hector them or browbeat them along the lines of my old drill sergeant who, when introducing himself to a new intake of fresh-faced recruits would scream 'My name is Sarn't Young. You will come to love me. And before you get any bright ideas about who runs this establishment, hear this. I am fire-proof, bomb-proof, water-proof and . . . always bleedin' right!'

Such techniques – especially the shout – are far more common today than I would have them. They may be effective enough for raking in the short-term buck; but I maintain that the long-term ten bucks is a more rational objective.

This argument, I know, cuts remarkably little ice with such flinthearted realists as accountants and managing directors who are governed by the constant necessity of ensuring that this year's figures are better than last year's. Their motto is: 'A buck in the hand is worth a dozen tentative enquiries. So to hell with the long-term benefits of advertising because, if we don't get that turnover up in something of a hurry, there won't *be* any long-term. Let's have some advertising that *sells*!' And by 'advertising that sells', they usually mean advertising that screams, hollers and stamps its feet such as no nicely brought up ad would ever do in public.

The offenders shriek: '*Save big, big money!*' or '*Astronomical bargains!*' or '*Fantastic, revolutionary supersavers!*' They treat us like halfwits; but we are not so halfwitted as to be unaware of that fundamental law of economics which states quite clearly that you only get what you pay for. So anyone who thinks he can bully us into believing that he runs some kind of charitable institution bent on handing out something for virtually nothing had better think again.

If (as maybe you unconsciously do) you indulge in a surplus of hyperbolics in your advertising copy, don't blame me if it fails to convince. No one likes a loud-mouth.

More to the point, no one believes a loud-mouth.

And even if he is grudgingly believed, when people find that his performance doesn't live up to his boasts, they will look with decided suspicion upon any future claims he may make. So, when he does come up with something worth shouting about, he is liable to get the big goodbye.

Therefore, don't ever shout unless you have something worth shouting about. If you do, you are liable to sound foolish; also people might detect the note of panic in your voice.

I must write a fable about this sometime; probably featuring a boy crying 'Wolf!'

Such advertising is unwise. In the long run (and most of us are in business as a long race) it is self-defeating; and it gives advertising the bad name it has and which, to be fair, it partly deserves.

The superlative

Somewhere – possibly somewhere south of Watford – there must exist an establishment called the splendid school of copywriting. There the eager-beaver students are brain-washed with adjective after purposive adjective . . . *dramatic . . . unbelievable . . . incredible . . . wonderful . . . magnificent . . . super.* Into their veins is injected the adrenalin of the superlative.

They emerge with glistening eye and impatient pen, to sprinkle their words and their themes like generous confetti over the world of fashion, furniture, cars, jewellery and the rest.

It's rather sad really to see all this effort and enthusiasm being pumped into ads that will be on a hiding to nothing in the believability stakes.

This again leads to hyperbole, but hyperbole of a different breed. The writers make a classic blunder in thinking that if they speak in flowery language, the grace of their prose will disguise the basic lack of product inform-ation.

They use such phrases as: '*A blend of style, elegance and excitement – a fashion mix of daring and distinction*'. And: '*Incomparably comfortable, breathtakingly beautiful and a masterpiece of unqualified excellence*'.

What does it all mean? Not very much, if you ask me. It says nothing whatsoever about the product that might even loosely be called tangible. You could use all of the above superlatives for anything from a pair of shoes to a three-piece suite, perm any eight from twenty-four, and nobody would be any the wiser – about anything.

It rings with all the conviction of a bell with no clapper.

Why do they do it? They do it because they believe they have a feel for words. Never mind about sales, they say. Let's show the world how fluent we are.

The mistake they make is in believing that people will actually take the trouble to digest their work. They won't. Listen – something like 70 per cent of the population has never taken the trouble to read Oscar Wilde – and they don't come much more superlative than he.

In addition to the one above, and not too far divorced from it, there exists a further school of advertising writing which I shall call the academy for business jargon. Its alumni pen ads for consumption by readers of the financial, business and semi-technical press – speaking to insurance brokers, electronics engineers, estate agents, solicitors, local authority engineers, and such.

Now I know that most of this is produced by ad agencies – but much isn't. And it isn't because the advertiser concerned reckons it is far too technical or complicated to be grasped by the average copywriter in the street. The consequence is, he writes it himself.

Frankly, I see no good reason why managing directors, advertising managers or business proprietors generally should not write their own stuff. After all, that's what this book is all about. But when one sees the outrages that are often perpetrated one begins to wonder.

'*Fully in tune with Britain's growing importance in the context of European markets*,' they waffle. '*Alert to the requirements of progressive industrial concepts,*' they burble. '*Serving an expanding economy with vigour and foresight,*' they prattle. '*Technical expertise combined with facilities for ongoing research and development,*' they jabber.

You don't believe it? Open any of the publications mentioned, as I just have, and see it for yourself.

Whatever your product or service, there must be something of factual interest you can say about it. Or, in the most unlikely event that there isn't, there are certainly more entertaining ways of saying nothing than this.

So the rule is, when you've something definite to say, say it straight. If you do, people understand you better.

The highly factual

Unless you are in the mail-order business where, for obvious reasons, everything that can be said about a product should be said in order to make the sale, it is totally unnecessary in the normal course of events to go into great and turgid detail about a product or service in your advertising. After all, the ad is only a vehicle for presenting a proposition which will draw enquiries; it is not attempting to make a sale. That happy event comes at a later date, if and when the prospect steps into your establishment or makes contact.

So never cram into an advertisement more than it will sensibly hold.

The most widely read ads, and the most carefully read ads, are those which set out the bare facts, then go on to whet appetites, implant curiosity, kindle desire.

The most carelessly read ads – though none are read with any real care – are those which set out to include everything bar the Dow Jones Index.

These jam-packed ads are somewhat reminiscent of EEC directives; and like EEC directives they are practically the most boring read one could contemplate.

They pile plump statistic upon plump statistic. They heap carefully nurtured fact upon carefully nurtured fact. They stack choice of colours upon sizes, upon weights, upon performance, upon ease-of-use, upon capacities, and upon anything else that crosses their mind at the time.

Apart from the obvious one of not getting read, there are two specific objections against writing ads in this vein.

The first is that if you can't argue with facts, what on earth can you argue with? So the more facts you offer for critical analysis, the more arguments you will have on your hands – or, if not on your hands, certainly in the mind of the reader. And if a reader can find one good excuse for doing absolutely nothing, via a fact he finds dubious, then he will do just that – absolutely nothing. The same applies to statistics. Being interpretable in any number of ways, they can also be contentious.

Most people, when thinking about a product for the first time, want to know little more than the absolute bare essentials – a well-framed outline of what is being offered. *Thereafter, what they require is a good reason, or set of reasons, for owning the thing.*

Give it to them.

★   ★   ★

Watch somebody leafing through a newspaper or magazine and you will witness a pattern of predictable events. The browser will thumb page after page, his eyes flickering hither and thither without alighting for any length of time on anything in particular. Then, all of a sudden, he will pause, stiffen almost imperceptibly, and incline his head towards the printed page. His attention will linger there for anything from a second or two to several minutes.

He has been hooked.

But what was it, in that great mass of words and pictures, that stood out from the rest like a large Scotch on a Temperance Hall tea trolley?

Well, that sort of naive question deserves a naive answer. I don't know, but then again I do.

Obviously, I can never know what will attract one individual to a specific item, simply because I have no idea what he likes, or what he believes in as an individual – nor, more importantly, what is on his mind at the moment my piece passes before his eyes.

I do know, however, from what feels like several hundred years of trying to come to a satisfactory conclusion about this very matter, that I can build into an ad an insurance against out-and-out rejection.

This insurance comes in the form of a five-point principle which can be 'offered up' to any ad and its rightness assessed. Here it is:

1   Has the headline/illustration combination the legs to walk the reader into the compass of the body copy?
    Would I, in all honesty, be drawn by either of them?
    Are they as good as, or better than, competitive lines and pictures which are likely to run alongside mine?
2   Is the body copy sufficiently well written to make it worth reading?
    Does it say something worth knowing?
    Does it inform?
3   Does the ad, overall, make an offer or give a promise?
    Is that offer or promise evident at first glance?
4   Is the USP presented with the emphasis it deserves?

Hold on, hold on! What's a USP? At risk of being labelled a graduate of the college of Laputa, I should tell those of you who don't already know that a USP is a unique selling proposition. That property which is deemed to be the single most important attribute of a product or service. And that which renders it *superior*, in one way or another, to *any other product or service currently available*.

However, the USP should not be confused, as it sometimes is, with benefit. A benefit of a product is what arises from its USP.

Let me put it this way.

Assume for a moment that you are in the business of manufacturing scaffold tube. Now, scaffold tube is, by any standards, heavy and cumbersome; and it is not such a product as one can tuck under one's arm and stroll away with. You, therefore, being one of nature's great metallurgists, have developed an ultra-light alloy from which you have, in turn, fabricated ultra-light tube. This tube is as strong and as durable as conventional tube, it costs exactly the same to make, yet length for length it weighs half as much.

So what, in this case, is the USP?

Is it the fact that the tube can be handled by one man instead of two or three? Is it that you can now load twice as much scaffold tube onto a truck – thereby cutting transport costs, or suggesting the use of smaller, less expensive vehicles? Is it that scaffolding can now be erected much faster than heretofore?

No. These are all *benefits*. Benefits to the user from owning the product.

The USP happens to be nothing more exciting than the relative lightness of the tube – with, perhaps, the peripheral properties of being just as strong and of comparable price.

In promoting the product, your major proposition would be something along the lines of: New Scaffolite is half the weight of ordinary scaffold tube. The difference means a big saving in time and money.

Every product or service, no matter what, has a definable USP. All you have to do is define it. Being sure, as you do so, that you latch on to that singular property which sets it apart from, and renders it in that specific quality more desirable than any similar product or service currently available.

But what if your product has no really unique sales point? Then you must try to present it in a unique way – in a way that will command attention and be totally different from your competitors' presentations.

*   *   *

The way I see it, advertising is at its very best when it demonstrates the product – when it shows how simply it . works, how quickly it works, or how effectively it works. This is accomplished in press adds with 'before-and-after' pictures, with pictures that compare the product with a similar product, and with 'exploded' diagrams.

Television, without doubt, is the most cogent medium for demonstration work. The cleverest of TV advertisers know this and exploit it for all it is worth.

I well remember the splendid demonstrations of the lawnmower manufacturers Qualcast and Flymo a year or two back. Even more vividly, I remember the marvellous verbal and visual attacks they made upon each other. The battle was all the more remarkable for being fought out in the living rooms of practically every household in the land. And the public loved it, because humour was there throughout and nobody appeared to be getting hurt. ('Knocking-type' advertising can often assume an ugly demeanour and develop into little more than slanging matches – which lose more on the swings than they gain on the roundabouts.)

Anyhow, the lawnmower skirmishes were demonstrative in every particular. For what it's worth, I think Qualcast came out the winner by a nose – though I can be persuaded otherwise, possibly by Messrs Flymo either delivering a free sample of their product or, at the very least, by undertaking to send someone round to mow my moss every fortnight for the duration.

So, where you can, give your audience a demonstration – and do it like this:

1   With a headline that announces or gives you a lead into the demonstration.
2   With a picture, or series of pictures, showing the product in action/its construction/a comparison with competitive products.
3   With body copy that spells out the demonstration message.

It doesn't require clever-cleverness, humour, or punning headlines. All you need for demonstration work is a straightforward, no-nonsense, down-to-earth approach which is so easy to understand that only a halfwit could confuse the issue.

★   ★   ★

It often happens – no, it usually happens – that most industrial advertisers and many retail advertisers, once they have run a campaign explaining the basic advantages of their product, think that their particular job has been done more or less for good and all. They see and see again their own ads plugging these basics; and they see their competitors' ads doing the same; and they come to the conclusion that the whole world knows about it and is rapidly tiring of hearing about these primary product properties.

This is a conclusion which is sometimes justified; but more often it is vastly mistaken. (As an aside, and I swear this is true, I recently came across a mature chap in full possession of his senses who didn't know what Polyfilla was. Maybe I exaggerate about the full possession bit because he was a remarkably stupid chap; but the moral is there all the same.)

Customers as a race are only about one-tenth as aware of your product or service as you think – and about one-twentieth as knowledgeable as you hope. There is, therefore, a lot to be said for keeping on plugging away at the simple, uncomplicated product-advantages or sales-proposition that you have to offer. If you have a campaign which projects them sensibly and forcibly, run it until you are absolutely *sure* that everyone is fed up to the back teeth with it. Then give it another twelve months for luck.

I reckon advertisers would be fairly taken aback if they went out and discovered the percentage of people in their marketplace who know absolutely nothing about them. I also think an abundance of them would be taken straight to the nearest asylum once they had calculated the cost of all that preaching to the indifferent – of all those messages falling upon deaf ears and blind eyes.

If I may use a musical analogy, I believe it was Dizzy Gillespie who once told a group of aspiring jazz musicians that if, in their improvisation of a melody, they hit upon a good phrase, they should repeat it and repeat it and repeat it. The point being that one half of the audience won't have taken it in at the first playing, and the half that did will be keen to hear it again.

Car dealers in particular seem to have a penchant for change for change's sake. All right, they have the financial and material backing of the manufacturer, via shared costs and pre-produced dealer blocks, so possibly they can afford to ring more changes. Yet even their own home-grown advertising assumes to broadcast too many messages over too short a period.

Should you even care, mine is the dubious distinction of having worked on more car dealership accounts than you could shake a lively stick at. Every single one of them, without exception, had a manic and contra-dracularian urge for 'something different' each time the sun rose. Give them a line that, in my judgement, would have the substance to work steadily for six months or more and they'd run it for a paltry few weeks. After which, they'd come back for more 'something differents'.

Which is a great way to confuse your market and to drive your designer and copywriter into an early-opening pub.

To quote a particular instance – when a competent ad I had written appeared for only a matter of days over a period of a fortnight and was then abandoned in favour of something different – how about this. The ad, to be honest, had produced a record number of enquiries for a very expensive product. Thus, when the client requested a change it was put to him that the success of the ad hardly pointed to the need for change.

'Agreed,' he replied, 'it has brought in plenty of enquiries, but it hasn't brought us a single order.'

The combined churlishness and illogicality of this attitude almost had me going home to cut my wrists. Maybe his product was wrong, his price was wrong, his salesmen were wrong or his method of handling enquiries was wrong; but it stood out that if one thing was *right* it was, in this case, the advertising.

The main object of the bulk of advertising is to produce *enquiries*. To expect it to attract direct and immediate orders is asking too much.

Good advertising can work wonders; but don't ask it to work miracles.

Anyhow, nobody should dash off believing that because they are bored with their advertising everybody else is.

You can see the wisdom of this by turning your mind to employment – or, rather, unemployment.

At the time of writing, the Government has introduced manifold schemes to help cut unemployment; and in one way or another, it has pushed these plans for all it's worth. We've had innumerable radio and television programmes on the subject. We've seen newspaper articles by the hundred. And we've witnessed the launching of advertising campaigns – along with promotional literature – to beat the band.

Were we reasonable, therefore, we might say that the Employment Secretary in particular, and various Ministers of the Crown in general, have done about as much as may be expected of the average bureacracy to put the message across.

Know what? Hardly one person in two has ever heard of more than a few of the thirty-one job training schemes currently available. This, despite a cool £3 billion being spent on the various projects annually, to say nothing of a £3 million advertising campaign currently on the go.

As a generalization, if an ad or a campaign is any good, it will almost certainly work for a damn sight longer than anyone closely connected with it supposes that it will. Infanticide is cruel; and unprofitable. (As epigrams go, this one may not make it into the *Oxford Dictionary of Quotations* – but its sentiments are none the less true.)

I rest my case

* * *

Will a coupon dramatically affect your response rate? Very probably. But the inclusion of a coupon in your advertising guarantees nothing unless the ad itself is sufficiently attractive, unless the reader is made to feel compelled to fill it in.

Speaking personally, I carry no torches for coupons, since most people always expect too much from them; and I hold that if a customer is determined enough to find out more about you, he or she, will do so without recourse to a coupon.

What's more, putting coupons in ads which are specifically addressed to upper echelon executives is a waste of space and effort. Indeed, many businessmen will be affronted by the implication that they have the time to mess around with them. If they are interested in you, they will instruct someone to phone or drop you a line – very rarely will they complete a coupon.

On a different level, though, the coupon has its uses. It helps to put your literature into the hands of respondents, or your representative into their homes; and it also furnishes names and addresses for future mail shots. But more importantly, it graphically indicates the effectiveness or otherwise of your advertising.

A good response, and you should stick with what you're obviously doing right. A bad response, or even a nil response – which heaven forfend – and it would be a good idea to organize something nasty for your writer and designer.

What kind of response should you expect from a coupon? Well, that all depends on whether you're asking as a client or a friend; but in the ordinary run of things don't anticipate more than 2.5 per cent of the publication's circulation – and even that would be a better than average comeback for an excellent ad placed in a specialist, low-wastage publication.

If the road to hell is paved with good intentions, then the road to a 100 per cent response is littered with coupons that people had every intention of filling in. Which is good enough reason, when you're looking for audience reaction, to switch to the Freefone device for prompting the customer to do something – now. The additional response may justify the extra expense.

But if you insist on a coupon, make sure it's a coupon of manageable proportions. There are those who can write the National Anthem on the back of a first-class stamp, yet there are a great number more who can't. Some coupons one comes across are too ridiculously small for their own good; and while I am a great believer that size (in anything) is not necessarily a measure of its effectiveness, it's clear that certain things can be taken too far – or made too microscopic. Also, word your coupon so as to give and to draw the maximum of information. Tell the punter what he may expect from you; and ask what you may expect of him. If you are sending a brochure, give its title. That way it will stand out from his junk mail as the one he requested. And always try to make space for three tick-boxes. One for a request for the brochure; one for whether he will entertain the proposition of a representative calling at his home; and one requesting permission to telephone him once he has received the brochure. (Don't, therefore, forget to include a space for his phone number.)

This may appear somewhat involved and a touch over the top. It isn't. A lot of people will refuse to see a salesman under any circumstances; and some won't willingly give their phone numbers; but most will allow you the courtesy of a telephone chat *if you ask first*.

Yet even if they deny both opportunities to you, their name is still on your file and you can prepare a follow-up mailing shot accordingly.

Incidentally, where you are appearing in more than one publication, you will be wise to code the various coupons – thus linking them to the publication in which they appear. Not to insult your intelligence, one way of doing this is by including a numeral or a capital letter in the corner of the coupon (a different one for each publication of course), or by prefixing your own address with a department number.

This way, once the ads have run and the coupons are in, you'll be in a position to judge which of the papers and magazines are working for you and which aren't.

You know what to do with the latter, don't you?

$$\star \quad \star \quad \star$$

It is my belief that if you have a story to tell, you can't beat words for telling it. The day of the big, beautiful picture with a very discreet line or two of copy at the bottom is, I think, dying. And, if it is, its death is a healthy symptom for business in general. Because, if what you've got to say takes more than a couple of dozen words (always assuming you are not writing for writing's sake) it implies that you have something worth saying. Which, in the case of a lot of advertisers, is a happy change.

Yes, I've seen lots of good ads in my time which conveyed a message in half a dozen words; but, by and large, these have either been half a dozen outstanding words or the ads in question have been for firmly established products and have been in the nature of reminders.

In general, I agree with whoever said: 'It's awfully hard to shift product without offering it for sale'.

4   Basic marketing practice

'Ours is a difficult product which presents special problems,' is a cry often heard in the land. This is seldom as true as one is led to believe.

Everyone – and I don't use the word lightly – everyone thinks that his or her own business is unusual or ultra-complicated. In advertising and marketing terms it rarely is. Not once you've raked over the problems and seived them down to manageable proportions, anyway.

And that's what marketing is all about.

The art of marketing may well be compared with the preparations one makes before taking a holiday abroad. You select the resort; book the hotel; buy an air-ticket; check that your passport is current; then pack your case and fill your wallet then, on the appointed day, make the journey.

Overlook a single one of these arrangements and the trip could turn out to be a bit of a disaster. By the same principle, when launching a new product or service, you disregard the common sense fundamentals of marketing at your considerable peril.

But there is no great mystery attached. I'll agree that when presented with a marketing buff in full flood, the simple mind might be forgiven for thinking that, by comparison, the theories of Albert Einstein are but rudimentary jottings. However, every trade has its jargon; and the degree of it is usually a sign of how seriously the people in it take their business. Anyway, in theory, the aim and purpose of marketing could be summed up something like this:

1   To develop the infinitely desirable product.
2   To discover the eternally insatiable market.
3   To forge a liaison between both.

In practice – and for our immediate purposes – what it amounts to is this:

1   You are sitting on a product or service. Who will buy it? Or:
2   There is a crying need for a so-and-so at such-and-such a price. Can you supply it?

So the first consideration when marketing a product is to establish whether there is a buying public for it. As someone so lucidly put it: '*There may very well be a gap in the market; but is there a market in the gap?*' Meaning that even if your product happens to be a clever variation of, and an improvement on, an existing one, you shouldn't delude yourself into believing that a market for same already endures. Equally, where you are introducing an innovative piece of goods that nobody has ever heard of, no matter how 'right' it seems, you will be very much obliged to create a need for it – instil the desire to own it.

The skateboard craze is a pertinent example. Kids have been riding on slabs of wood placed across a rollerskate ever since the rollerskate was invented. (I know, because I used to do it.) Yet it required marketing genius to take an idea that had been around, however sparsely distributed, for many years and develop it into the universal mania which prevailed for a profitable while.

The market gap for skateboards had been wide open for decades; and I don't doubt for a moment that someone long ago had considered filling it. His initial research would have shown, though, that he'd be wasting his effort, since in that day and age only a handful of youngsters could afford tō buy skates never mind a cosmetic variant.

Consequently – gap, but no market.

The second part of this marketing-gospel-according-to-me which we must consider, is discovering where our market lies in the earnings league – in order to sell into it the more easily. The word 'sell', here, does not apply to pricing exclusively. It is also very relevant to the sales strategy and creative stance you will employ, i.e. the language and the atmosphere of your advertising.

Sadly, the pursuit of education is not nearly so popular as some other activities I could mention. A number of people refuse it point-blank; others are denied it by force of circumstances. So it follows that there are many who are neither as scholarly nor, if I may make so bold, as well read as you so clearly are, sir or madam. Couple this with the bogglingly obvious disclosure that a meagre education usually denotes a poor or less than wealthy background and you have all the ingredients for class distinction.

Socio-economic class distinction, to coin a well-worn phrase.

Now, I am not about to be drawn into lengthy discussions on socio-economic groupings, disposable and discretionary incomes, and all of that. In any case, I don't know enough about it and I should only end up by making myself look foolish. You can glean everything you want to know from a variety of specialist books – and you could do infinitely worse than work your way through the 'Marketing Series', published by William Heinemann with the Institute of Marketing. Each of them is written by an authority in a particular field and you are bound to find your special pasture among them.

For this present exercise, though, too much erudition might well be a dangerous thing; so I suggest we do no more than look at markets from a common sense viewpoint. This viewpoint is the one adopted by sensible advertising executives when 'briefing' an agency's creative people on the level at which to pitch their advertising message – the level at which it will be understood by the market in question.

To achieve this, everyone in the entire population is given a rating from A to E. A represents the upper echelon, while E stands for the lowest income bracket. Here's the scale explained more fully.

A   *Upper middle class*
     Professional people. Corporation chairmen. Top
     management.
B   *Middle class*
     Intermediate management. Airline pilots. Farmers.
     MPs.
C1   *Lower middle class*
     Supervisory or clerical personnel. Nurses. Sales
     representatives.
C2   *Skilled working class*
     Mechanics. Printers. Carpenters. Machinists. Brick-
     layers.
D   *Working class*
     Semi-skilled and unskilled workers. Bus conductors.
     Canteen staff. Labourers.
E   *Lowest level of subsistence*
     Casual workers and people living on state pensions.

These are by no means hard and fast definitions, since
there is a degree of overlap throughout the list. But for the
purposes of quickly assessing where your market lies it
cannot be equalled.

Look at it this way. You are launching an extremely
expensive, hand-made leather briefcase. Who in the list is
likely to use a briefcase? Who will need one? Who can afford
yours? Answer: the A, B, C1 grouping. On the other hand,
you have a range of cheap, but colourful luggage made
from synthetic fabrics. Where's the market? Clearly, it's
C1, C2, D.

All you have to do now is determine where the pertinent
markets can be located, and you're home and dry. What
newspapers and magazines do they habitually read? Which
TV programmes and radio stations do they tune into?

Again, common sense is the key. The chairman of an oil
conglomerate is hardly likely to turn to the *Sun* or the *Daily
Mirror* for informed reporting on matters that affect him –
like overseas affairs and stock prices, for instance. He is
more liable to go for *The Daily Telegraph* or *The Financial
Times*. Conversely, your average machine-minder, with no

gilt-edged securities to speak of and with no overseas investments worth talking about, will almost certainly be a tabloid reader. He also won't read *Field* or *Oilman* on a regular basis, but he may well come into steady contact with publications like the *Angling Times* and *Exchange & Mart*.

As I say, there are overlaps. Rumour has it that a very eminent MP is a regular reader of *Beano*. Knowing the man, I am not the least bit surprised. Were I to reveal his name, you wouldn't be greatly staggered, either. But, generally speaking, you can pin down your market by a careful study of the media available; and if you find the odd politician within your sphere of things, consider it a bonus.

Media can be studied quite readily and very simply. Every publication worthy of being read produces an 'advertising pack' consisting of insertion rates, circulation figures, and readership breakdown. You just have to phone or write to the advertising manager concerned and request these documents. For a comprehensive list of newspapers, periodicals, radio and TV stations to whom to write, lay your hands on a copy of *British Rates & Data* (BRAD) at any central lending library; or, if you're feeling in an extravagant mood, lash out £70 and get it direct from 76 Oxford Street, London W1N 9FD. (Phone: 01 434 2233.) Information contained in BRAD is priceless; so a little digging and delving will put you on the right track for an unerring shot at your audience.

★   ★   ★

And now for a sweeping generalization. It is a fallacy to suppose that you can sell a product or a service on price alone. More specifically, stripping prices to the bone with the object of undercutting competitors' prices, frequently has the opposite effect to the one desired.

The psychology of the average Janet and John in the street is such that if you hand them something on the cheap they will, more often than not, regard it as a cheap something – a less than good something, a something of little importance.

The true value to the customer is not being reflected in the price.
The result of this is that fewer customers purchase the
thing, because it has no significant value to them.

In marketing jargon, underpricing is called opport-
unity-forfeited risk. Which may, in turn, lead to loss-risk,
i.e. where revenue falls below production/selling costs, but
where prices cannot be increased on account of the public
refuses to buy that previously *cheap* item at an inflated price.
The moral is: when you sow the seed of worthlessness, you
must be prepared to reap the bitter harvest.

Cosmetics, or rather, certain cosmetics, are a case very
much in point. I would be prepared to wager that many
handcreams can be manufactured for around £15 a hundred-
weight. Yet assessing it from its retail price per jar, the
implied value is something approaching £1000 a hundred-
weight. Manifestly, was this stuff to be priced according
to its true worth, the product would be of small value to the
consumer. All the mystery would go out of it – especially
that mystery which is usually attached to the formula of
such substances. After all, rare herbs are costly, aren't they?
Never mind that the rare herb content might be one part per
million.

Consequently, a large number of women would then
prefer the unsightliness (or so they suppose) of red hands to
the nasty business of slapping 'muck' on them. All right, as
it stands handcream is still muck, but it's desirable muck;
and it is this desire which keeps a multi-million pound
industry gainful.

A close friend of mine is in the car-repair business, but
car-repair with a difference. This chap works solely on
upper price-bracket British and foreign vehicles – high
performance and sports cars in the main. He is an un-
doubted expert in his field and, by doing what he's doing,
has cut himself a large wedge of a highly profitable pie.

However, it wasn't always thus. When he first went into
business, he tried to attract custom by undercutting the
prices charged by others similarly engaged. His pricing was
around one-third of theirs. Despite this obvious benefit, the
business had little momentum; he found, as others who

have followed similar courses have found, that only a handful of customers were attracted to his establishment.

What was he doing wrong? Did he not know these machines inside out? And did he not perform conscientiously, with care and speed?

Too true, he did. But what he had failed to understand was that cars are a stress purchase. Motorists who had paid upwards of £25,000 for a car, and who possibly loved it more profoundly than they loved their mothers, were not about to punt around looking for cheap servicing deals. Neither were they all that sanguine about handing over their prized auto to a chap who worked on the cheap and, by implication, on the bodgy side.

With nothing to lose, this very bright spark took some advice (mine, if you want to know) and doubled his prices; thus charging a third again what the regular garages were invoicing.

I am here to tell you that he has never looked back. So much so, he has just invested in his first Rolls Royce.

'They enjoy being stung,' he grins. 'I could have given them exactly the same job for half the price, but they just wouldn't wear it. Can you fathom that?'

Frankly, no – but that's the way it happens to be. Anyone who supposes, therefore, that he will make a killing by selling cheap will most probably sell himself short.

* * *

The third marketing ponderable is that of clearly defining your market and, thereafter, selecting the media through which to approach it.

You may believe that the markets for the great proportion of products speak for themselves; and in all probability you are right. In which case, very little groundwork is called for.

A small-town TV and video dealer, say, would be wise to put most of his advertising into a year-round programme of well-written ads in the local press with, maybe, the occasional in-showroom promotion to help push new models or to shift a backlog of old ones.

But let's assume you run a small joinery firm which has developed an innovative line in solid timber, reproduction Louis XIV chess tables. Let's also go on to assume that you can knock out said tables at a pretty rapid rate and at a very reasonable price: say, two-dozen units a day at a cost to you of £20 each. For the sake of completing the picture, the tables have a chessboard inlaid and are finished to a high standard.

In any event, they come in a 'knock-down' format and can be assembled by the customer, without recourse to screws or glue, in a matter of minutes. Thus, the product can be delivered to the consumer in one neat package.

So do you sell the said table directly to the consumer via mail-order advertising, or do you find outlets by way of retail chain-stores, furniture shops and warehouses? Or could it be a combination of both?

Before you do anything, you must come to some conclusions about the following:

1   *Basic selling price*
    This will be arrived at from calculations of your materials, production, packaging, administration and promotional costs. With due regard – you'd better believe it – to the retail price of furniture of a comparable quality.
2   *Colour range*
    Whether or not the chessboard element of the table should be available in a choice of wood stains.
3   *Packaging*
    The virtues of packing the tables in decoratively printed or plain cardboard containers.
4   *Carriage*
    Should it turn out that you'll be selling by direct mail, what are the postage costs?

Nobody but you can resolve these matters; but purely for pig iron, let's do a rough costing on this example to see what a basic selling price would look like. We shall base it on a production output of twenty-four units a day for 48 weeks, i.e. 5760 chess tables per annum. The £30 unit cost

includes wages and all production overheads. Total
production cost over the year is therefore £172,800.

Now we'll break it down.

Packaging is a simple but tough cardboard outer, while
administration and handling costs are based on one
employee earning £100 a week.

	Per unit
Production costs	£30.00
Packaging	2.50
Administration	.84
	£33.34
Carriage	3.60
	£36.94
Mark up @ 33⅓%	12.32
	£49.26

Just one more ingredient to include, your advertising and
promotional costs. But how do we arrive at a sensible
budget?

Well, on the figures given, your gross turnover per
annum will be £283,737. In an earlier chapter, I said that 10
per cent of net income was a reasonable advertising budget
guideline. Thus, with a projected net income amounting to
£70,963, the arbitrary 10 per cent represents £7,096.

Now that may seem like a great deal of cash, and it is; but
reflect on what it will be asked to accomplish. First, it must
pay for the printing of 'assembly instructions' leaflets – after
all, your customers need to be told how to put the thing
together. Second, it has to launch the product on to the
market via press, radio and what have you. In these terms, it
amounts to very little.

Of course, the £7,096 budget must now be *incorporated*
into the basic selling price. Which adds £1.23 to each unit –
resulting in an all-up unit price of £50.49.

It looks to me like a good case for marking up to £59.99 per table. What do you say?

By jacking up the price like so, we shall make an extra £9-odd profit per unit. I would certainly not be inclined to mark it down to £49.99, however psychologically acceptable that price may appear. Not until I had market tested it at the higher price, at any rate. And without thinking about it too deeply, I would spend quite a proportion of that extra profit on advertising, with the prospect of creating more orders and to help promote growth of the company.

Anyway, that's roughly how to go about costing out a new product. But please, I beg of you, don't take any of these figures as gospel, nor the methods for arriving at them as holy writ. These are much-simplified templates for a hypothetical case. For the real McCoy formulae, consult those marketing books as suggested a few pages back.

It all needs very careful consideration; but if you are cute, you might invite your regional development agency to take a look at your particular marketing strategy and ask for some sound advice. I understand that these agencies are pretty much alive to marketing problems.

So, having come to a tentative decision on selling price, what you must now do is run a test-marketing exercise. In other words, you undertake a bit of research to plumb·the extent of the market.

But, first, what *is* the market for a decently-produced chess table? I don't suppose I'd be far off the mark if I said that your chess table doesn't mind who buys it – just so long as it gets bought. However, you need a fair idea of who might buy it, so that you can present it to them the more efficiently.

It occurs to me that chess isn't such a game as you could call highly popular among the masses. So to try to sell the table as a functional chess item, to the exclusion of all else, would certainly be a mistake. The message that our table could 'make your chess-playing life a real pleasure' would go right over the heads of those who can't, or don't as a general rule, play. Which must encompass a good two-thirds of the population.

On the other hand, the table is a nice-looking piece of furniture which will appeal to many people throughout the socio-economic spectrum. More precisely, it should appeal to the lower end of the B ratings and to the higher portion of the C2s – taking in all of the C1s.

This, I should make it clear, is no more than guesswork and would require serious substantiation. However, it is specific enough for our present purposes.

Now back to gauging the extent of the market.

First, you mail or visit those chain-stores, furniture shops and warehouses, presenting your sample and your *written* proposition to the senior buyer in each case. This will quickly show how eager, or otherwise they are to handle your product.

And that, since it involves only your time, is the cheapest form of market testing.

If you, like very many of us, find it difficult to go out and sell yourself, eyeball-to-eyeball – especially to hard nosed, professional buyers who eat amateur salesmen for breakfast – please allow me to recommend the definitive work on 'selling in'. Written by super-salesman Tony Adams, it's titled *The Secrets of Successful Selling*; and it is published, like all good books are published, by William Heinemann.

The more expensive method of verifying your market, but arguably the most profitable, because you are cutting out the middle men, is to run a series of feeler ads, direct selling ads, aimed expressly at the consumer. The response to this effort would settle once and for all your future marketing policy.

Now these don't have to be big, bold, full-colour weekend magazine type ads – not, that is, until you have assessed consumer response and found it begging for more.

Apart from anything else, at the time of writing, a full-page, full-colour ad in *You* (the *Mail on Sunday* supplement) will cost from £9,800 upwards. And that's for one insertion only.

No, sir – the way to play it is this. Investigate space costs in a selection of regional daily and weekly newspapers; and choose those papers which are circulated in the more prosperous areas of the country. Papers which are seen by a predominance of B; C1 and C2 rated readers. And for blanket coverage of these groups take a good, close look at the regional editions of publications like *Radio Times* and *TV Times*. These can be bought by the region and are not beyond the pocket of the small-budget advertiser, since a quarter page black-and-white can cost as little as £110 per insertion. Top of the price-range is the London region at £1,150 for a quarter page.

In any event, for a test-marketing exercise, you will buy the largest spaces you can afford; and it is imperative that your ad contains as much information as it will sensibly hold – including a good picture.

What you are doing, in essence, is selling 'off-the-page'. You will be asking people to send money on the basis of the information you present to them. For this reason, everything that can be said about the product should be said: the price, the dimensions; the materials; the colour; the ease of assembly; delivery period; methods of payment – the lot.

And a coupon is mandatory.

Spend a bit of time browsing the 'off-the-page' ads of the larger mail-order houses and book clubs in order to assess copy style and coupon format. These are written and produced to a formula which has been tried-and-tested over many years. It works for them, so it will work for you.

Any promotional activity should not, most definitely not be restricted to advertising alone. It would be prudent, to say the least, to make one hell of a hullabaloo in the public relations field, also.

As far as I can gather, all trade publications and special interest magazines have some kind of 'new product/ test-bench' page, the primary purpose of which is to introduce readers to up-and-coming products. You can get yourself featured on new product pages – and into the public domain – by soliciting the editors in question. Off the cuff, I would say that our chess table would find a ready slot in magazines such as *Good Housekeeping*, *The Lady*, and a whole host of women's interest publications; along with papers like *Do-It-Yourself*, *Practical Householder* and so forth. More about that in Chapter 6.

At any rate, successful marketing revolves around the principle of paying minute attention to what the purchaser requires. This is known as the *demand philosophy* and, as such, determines what can and cannot be sold. I would venture to suggest that half of the battle is to be able to look at your business from *the customer's point of view*.

If you need a formula for successfully marketing a new product, I offer the following in relation to our chess table.

Objective	Consumer	Trade
Analysing the market		
Identify the market opportunity and estimate the total possible sales.	Taking a cross-section, how many people would be prepared to buy such a table? And in which socio-economic grouping do those people lie?	What is the turnover of 'novelty' furniture products per year in a sample of chain-stores and warehouses?
Testing the concept		
Establish the desire to purchase	How many of the above would invest in a chess table after its qualities are demonstrated?	How many of the above would be prepared to stock the table 'sale or return'; and in what quantities?
Developing the product		
Identify the manufacturing 'quality' that the target market expects.	How much will they pay? How should it be packaged? Must it come in a range of finishes? Calculate costs of selling by direct mail.	Establish retailers' profit margins.

Advertising and promoting the product		
Determine how to approach the target market. Develop an advertising platform and strategy.	Which media will most effectively reach this audience? Press, radio, television?	Develop an advertising/ mailing/direct-selling campaign to reach this market.

Armed with the answers to all these questions, you should have amassed enough information to conclude exactly where the market (if any) lies and how you can reach it.

I make no bones about it, finding the answers is considerably more difficult than it appears. Whatever the product, what you have to do – and there's no alternative – is get on the phone, or jump on the bus, and go out and ask. Or, as we said with the chess table, run a feeler campaign in the press.

When quizzing the general public, consider the idea of hiring a small, hotel functions room. The hotel would, ideally, be situated in a main street; and you could try persuading passers-by to go inside and take a comfortable seat while you put the questions to them. Without a shadow of doubt, women make far the best interrogators in this context. Female 'researchers' can be recruited from any decent model agency – but you must give them a thorough briefing before sending them out onto the street.

I remember once being dragged off the street into, of all things, an orange juice sampling survey, by a most attractive young lady. She plied me with orange juice of all shades, flavours and textures; but I may tell you that orange juice was the last thing on my mind. Sadly, nothing came of it.

However, as in most things, the women have the edge. Before you visit retailers, it is advisable to make an appointment. Do this by phone or, with possibly more chance of success, by letter. Such a letter could also carry sales literature or photographs of the product. If this fails to fetch a response, mail them again, then phone promptly.

My knowledge of 'selling-in' to retailers might reasonably be described as scanty, and my ideas on the subject would doubtless reduce the tutors of the Harvard Business School to uncontrollable tears. Nevertheless, common sense tells me that buyers are human beings after all and, like the rest of us, can be persuaded by any argument which promises rich pickings.

So my advice is, give them an argument.

★　　★　　★

Let's suppose that you have properly identified your market, and let's also assume that you have allocated an advertising budget with which to reach it. What now? Now we must take a good, long look at your business and slot it into one of the following categories.

1　Is your product or service a seasonal one? Are you limited to catching sales at one specific time of the year?

　　Into this category would fall: winter clothing; Christmas cards; garden furniture; horticultural products, and so on.

2　Does it have a year-round market? Like office equipment, hand tools, furniture, electrical goods, legal and estate agency services?

3　Or is it mainly seasonal, with a moderate market out of season? I'm thinking, here, of things like plumbing services, quarry supplies, hotel accommodation and self-drive car hire.

Providing that your business falls into one or other of these categories – and thinking about it, there's no way it won't – you can now establish the frequency of your advertising.

For number one, above, it's self-evident that you should advertise just prior to and during the particular seasonal period. What's more, you do so in the largest spaces the budget will stretch to.

For number two, you drip-feed the ads on a regular basis throughout the twelve months. Making the necessary allowances, of course, for national and trades holidays. There's no future in directing a message at an audience which has folded its tent and slipped away to Blackpool for a couple of weeks. Because of the extent of the advertising period, these ads should be in smaller spaces – so they will have to work harder.

Number three is a combination of the first two: big splashes during the season, with a series of reminder ads spread throughout the remainder of the year.

I should make it clear that these are nothing more than guidelines which need to be carefully interpreted. As a straightforward example of what I'm getting at, it's logical that with some seasonal enterprises it is sometimes necessary to advertise *well in advance* of the availability of the product or service. And I cite the holiday industry as a classic. The package holiday trade issues its brochures and belts out its advertising in January for a product that may not be used for several months.

Hitting the target market when it is most susceptible to your overtures is all important in advertising – in fact, it's crucial.

So, like the holiday industry, which grabs people at a time when they are up to here with rain, sleet, snow and ice and are more than ready to talk sun and swimming pools, you must be seen to be around when you are needed.

To help you get your timing right, and as a way of providing yourself with a total picture of your advertising campaign 'at a glance', you may wish to compile a schedule along the following lines.

Advertising schedule

Publication	Size	Jan.	Feb.	Mar.	Apr.	May	Jun.	Jul.	Aug.	Sept.	Oct.	Nov.	Dec.	Cost per insertion	Total
Home Furnishings (monthly)	½p		X		X	X	X							£540	£2,160
Beautiful Homes (weekly)	¼p	10	7	14	18	9			25	12	17	14	3	£375	£3,750
Furniture Buyer (quarterly)	½p	X			X			X			X			£680	£2,720
														Total:	£8,530

The monthly and quarterly publications usually appear on the first of the month in question.

The above schedule must not be taken as an actual proposition, since the publications are totally fictitious and the insertion dates purely arbitrary. None the less, I think it gives you the general idea.

*   *   *

Now a word about the role that certain aspects of marketing can play in revitalizing an ailing business, or one which is forced into a corner by a local price war.

Put yourself in the position, please, of a small, traditional printer who sees his business declining due to the fierce competition from cut-rate 'rapid printing' services. He might recognize that he is on the skids and feel like jacking it all in. After all, these new outfits are equipped with modern photoprinting technology and thus armed can leave him standing on the price of general jobbing printing. So his normally brisk trade in one or two-colour letterheads, compliments slips and such is going swiftly down the Shanks.

What they cannot beat him at, and will never have a hope of beating him at, is colour printing. Neither on price, nor on quality.

There are two courses of action open to our printer. He can either approach the instant printing firms and offer them a colour printing service – which they are pretty much unable to provide off their own bat. Or he can methodically undercut the competition on black-and-white jobbing work, deliberately taking a loss, while balancing that loss with a good profit from the colour jobs.

One or other of these ploys will at least maintain him in business.

And here's a further thought. A couple of hours spent examining the records at the local companies house will tell our man everything he needs to know about his competitors' profitability. All he has to do is examine their annual accounts; and an analysis of the information gleaned will decide him on whether to join forces with them, or play a waiting game in the hope of their collapse coming sooner rather than later.

Should he decide to take the second course, he might bolster his own profits somewhat by stocking and selling stationery-related products of interest to his existing customers. Things like filing systems, binders, typewriter ribbons – even office hardware such as filing cabinets and furniture. The current customers for his colour printing are, quite clearly, thriving businesses which would benefit from such a service. Not only that, they happen to represent a ready-made and partisan market.

If this teaching-of-grandmothers cameo is a mite puerile for your palate, ponder the not so simplistic problem which confronts the modest-sized plastics-moulding firm.

This company produces, among other things, plastic products for the transmission of surface water (guttering and pipework) and for underground drainage and effluent systems (inspection chambers, manhole bases, bottle gullies) – all of which is sold direct to construction firms, or indirectly via plumbers' merchants.

So far, so good.

Yet competition is fierce; and when all is said and done, the company can only sell so much pipework in a given season. Therefore, if they desire growth, they must either diversify into other plastics fields – involving costly re-tooling – or remain in the business they are in and try to sell harder.

But what business *are* they in? Plastics components manufacture, or the building supplies trade?

Can you think of any good reason why they shouldn't sell building equipment made by other firms; and sell it direct to their established, construction trade clients?

Neither can I. And it seems to me to be the best course for expanding their business, and increasing their profits, without having to lash out on expensive plant and capital equipment.

As I said earlier, marketing is largely a matter of using what you, sir or madam, so patently have a lot of – otherwise you wouldn't be reading this book.

It's called common sense.

★   ★   ★

In the marketing game, knowledge is power. Too many small companies have too little intelligence of what their competitors are doing and what the market is thinking. Like: 'Oh, if only we could get all our such-and-such supplies from one outlet, instead of having to patronize two or three different firms.' So the person who bothers to get up out of his seat and ask the questions is streets ahead in the information stakes, and well on top in the power struggle.

As anyone who knows me will tell you, I am no great advocate of research, especially predictive research – that which sets out to prove in advance whether a particular advertising concept will, or will not, fetch results. There is no one on God's earth capable of accurately prophesying the likely outcome of, say, a series of ads or a batch of commercials. Research, in this context, can only tell you whether your *last* campaign was, or was not, successful. That's all. Research should be treated with the circumspection it deserves, I always say.

But research as a means of plumbing the depths of a given market, or accumulating information about rivals, is a dog of another breed. In a word, it's invaluable.

Value it.

★   ★   ★

Preparing a mailing list

You can compile a comprehensive mailing list of potential customers in a variety of uncomplicated ways.

1   *From the Yellow Pages and business directories.*
    Just let your fingers do the walking, and your brain the selecting of companies you would wish to mail. You'll find the necessary books at your local post office or public library.
2   *From the electoral roll.*
    This really speaks for itself; and you can examine the list at public libraries or relevant council offices.
3   *From the coupon response to your own ads.*

4   *From Dun & Bradstreet.*
    This is one of the largest and best respected of all the
    firms which earn their livings by selling specialist
    mailing lists.
5   *From the Chamber of Commerce National Directories.*
    Here you'll find Chambers of Commerce and their
    member companies, countrywide. Copies can be seen
    in any central public library.

5 The press, print and production

We are, of course, all aware that editors of newspapers and magazines never, ever allow considerations of advertising to influence a single word they print.

Ask any editor.

But we are also equally aware that an editorial of any size on a company or product invariably lies cheek by jowl with a big piece of advertising for the company or product so featured. Since I was brought up to believe every word that editors speak, I can only put this down to some vast and continuing coincidence.

It might well be argued that these are cases not of editorial being influenced by advertising, but of advertising being influenced by editorial. Then again, I don't believe in fairies either.

However, let's not get all worked up and unreasonable about this. Publishing is a business, not a religion; and I for one see no harm in a little *quid pro quo* of this nature.

The concept of: 'I write about your company, you buy my advertising space,' seems to me a tolerable one – provided that it is kept within sensible bounds. And it usually is; although there are one or two papers I could name, if I were not afraid of being sued, which make too much of a habit of it.

Is the above as instructive a parable to you as it ought to be? If not, allow me to make it gin clear. When dealing with the press – when paying it good money to reproduce your advertising on its pages – never forget to ask whether they will back your ads with a touch of supporting editorial. So when you take a half-page in the *Glasgow Leatherworkers Clarion*, try to talk them into filling up the remaining half of the page with a thousand or so well-chosen words about you, your company and your product. That way, you get two half-pages for the price of one.

But let's start this section where I should have started it: at the beginning.

Newspapers and periodicals provide a relatively inexpensive service for the small-business advertiser (relative to radio and television, that is). Generally speaking, they do a sterling job; the more so when you consider the junk, both visual and verbal, they are asked to reproduce.

Just like everyone else, the press is in business to make a profit and, almost without exception, they survive on the revenue generated by advertising. Very few editors these days are able to run a viable paper on cover-price alone. For all I know, none can. They simply cannot furnish editorial content which is interesting enough in itself ever to make advertising content a bonus, let along make it redundant.

Thus, when you approach the advertisement manager of a publication and wave fistfuls of negotiable currency under his nose, he will understandably hope that you are one of those who is, proverbially, begot every sixty seconds. To ascertain whether this is so, he will regale you with a well rehearsed speech about his paper's circulation, about the cost-per-thousand readership, about opportunities to see, and about how foolish you would be not to accept the bargain his paper so patently represents.

He will, in other words, quite properly try to sell you the maximum amount of space at the highest cost.

All right, I guess we all have our *bête noire*, but some *noires* are more *bête* than they sensibly ought to be. Meaning that if you can't stand the thought of haggling and allow yourself to be sold in this manner, you deserve everything you get. Which will almost certainly be a fatter invoice than what it might be if you are prepared to negotiate.

Every newspaper and periodical issues a rate card. This document is a tariff of charges for the various kinds of space available; and there are different rates for different types of space. These can be grouped under three main headings: display; semi-display; and classified.

Here's a mock-up of a rate card showing what you may expect to find:

LAMANCHA ECHO

Standard rates (per single column centimetre)	£6
Special rates:	
Full page:	£1,680
Guaranteed position:	25% extra
Front page solus (15 cm × 2 columns):	£430
Solus centre news page (20 cm × 3 columns):	£450
Title corners (front page: 4.8 cm × 4.8 cm):	£65
Page three (per single column centimetre):	£8

Colour rates. Spot colour 15% extra on standard rate.

Classified advertisements:
Trade and professional £1.85 (minimum 3 lines).

Cash discounts: 10% cash discount for settlement within 14 days of despatch of invoice.

Mechanical data: Column length: 400 mm; width 38 mm. Number of columns: 7. Screen: 26. Same size camera-ready artwork required.

Even this much-simplified example shows that you need your wits about you when buying space. Note the different rates for special positions (the 'title corners' mentioned are the ear-spaces positioned on either side of the paper's front-page masthead or title.) A rate card should also give the discount available for a series of ads, and for buying space in a number of publications in a newspaper group.

More about space later. Right now, allow me to draw your attention to the matter of circulation figures and readership figures.

The circulation figure issued by a publication refers to the number of copies printed and distributed. Among these will be many 'voucher' or presentation copies, plus any number unsold on the sale-or-return arrangement. These, from the advertiser's point of view, are wasted copies. The readership figure, on the other hand, represents the total number of times each copy of the paper is read.

Clearly, a paper brought into a household can be seen by more people than just the purchaser. So, in reality, there are two readership figures. The first denoting the individuals who have bought copies (net sales), while the second is total readership.

Much research is undertaken in this area; yet it is as well to bear in mind that the latter is never hard-and-fast, it being a quantity arrived at from statistical assumptions.

Which leads us on to the similarly obscure consideration of the 'opportunities-to-see', or OTS, figure – the total number of times your advertising *can* be seen.

Run a single ad, or a series of ads, over a period and the OTS figure must certainly be greater the longer it runs, or if it appears in more than one publication. Thus, OTS is roughly the total readership per publication issue, multiplied by the number of times your ad appears. But there will be a good proportion of wastage because the opportunity isn't always taken; and this manifests itself by: (a) an overlap of readers between one publication and another; (b) a reluctance on the part of readers to read the same ad twice; (c) the fact that some readers of the paper may not notice your ad at any time; (d) a refusal by some to read advertising out of principle.

All of which, I would say, presents a striking case for ringing the changes when considering a campaign of *any duration*. A campaign consisting of a series of different-looking ads, but which contain essentially the same message, will definitely enjoy a larger readership figure than a campaign of the same duration employing only one ad. In this respect, the 'entertainment value' of a series is priceless. If you can imbue your material with that quality whereby the market is amused to the point of enjoying each subsequent ad, then your actual readership figure may even come close to matching the forecasts of an over-optimistic advertisement manager.

It doesn't require a genius to figure out that circulation and readership can be juggled to give a more acceptable picture. (This is just as true of listenership and viewership figures.) And they now and again are. The prospective advertiser should therefore treat all claims with a little circumspection; although if these are backed by the researches of that august body ABC – the Audit Bureau of Circulation – then you can pretty much rely on them.

Adorning every rate card, too, there is likely to be a cost-per-thousand-readership figure. From what we've already seen, this should be calculated on readership, not on circulation. So the cost to you per one-thousand readers, is the cost of your advertising space divided by the true readership.

So far so good. But how many among the readership will fall into the range of your target audience? How many will be in the market for what you are offering; and how many won't? Better still, how much of that cost-per-thousand will you be chucking down the drain? Good question.

It is the ability to precisely pin-point target audiences that makes ad agency media buyers the indispensable and highly rewarded people they are. This, combined with their penchant for haggling and buying space at preferential rates, is why they are so well respected within the industry. But I maintain that anyone who has taken the trouble to gather all the necessary facts and figures can, relatively speaking, do a comparable job and be just as effective at identifying exactly where markets lie.

Before making any commitments, therefore, get all the facts and figures. More specifically, demand a readership 'profile' from every publication you may think of using. This presents a breakdown of the socio-economic status, demographic location, occupations and interests of the readership. Such a precaution is important even when you are evaluating two publications which appear to be catering for identical audiences – like, say, two general aviation magazines. On the face of it, the publications *Pilot* and *Aeroplane Monthly* are aimed at the same audience. Both carry feature articles on the test-flying of aircraft; both include stories about international flights undertaken by readers – complete with flight plans and airport inform- ation; and both produce cameos of aviation personalities.

A close scrutiny of readership profile, however, shows unmistakeably that *Pilot* attracts a greater number of student pilots, while *Aeroplane Monthly* is geared towards experienced flyers and commercial and military airmen.

Irrespective of their individual circulation figures (*Aeroplane Monthly* is the larger by around 10,000), it is perfectly clear that should you be selling products of appeal to students – flying training manuals, for instance – you would choose *Pilot* as your medium. Large circulation and large readership means nothing unless your target market is specifically located within that readership. You could advertise your training manuals in *Aeroplane Monthly* until you were blue in the face and you would never draw the responses that *Pilot* could give – even though the latter has a smaller readership and could, in certain circumstances, cost more per thousand readers.

So by all means listen to what the advertisement manager has to say; but by no means be sold without first checking the figures.

What about the horse-trading I mentioned earlier?

I address myself now to those who will be spending most of their budget in the technical and industrial media. You *can* do deals, and you *should* do deals. Allowing that you may be appearing in a trade magazine upwards of a dozen, or even several dozen times a year, don't simply be content with the normal series discount? To start with, most trade magazines are hungry – very hungry; and you'll know how badly they need your business by how quickly they send you the requested rate card, and how quickly they follow it up with a: 'Can we be of any further assistance, sir or madam,' telephone call.

At which point, you should mention your budget, but appear undecided about who to spend it with and are hovering between them and some other publication, which you should name. Be careful that the one you mention is not from the same publishing stable, otherwise they won't bite.

In this way are bargains struck and rates reduced. Like this, you can win yourself an extra ad insertion or three, for the same money.

As I've written elsewhere, I know of one media man who earns more for his by-no-means small ad agency by wheeling and dealing than any other ten people on the payroll. If someone of such professionalism and implied respectability can get away with it, you can certainly get away with it.

★   ★   ★

I should be even more of a bore than I already am, were I to tell you that the positioning of your ads in publications is quite material in the battle to get them noticed. Nevertheless, it happens to be true.

What, then, is a good position?

Observe someone idly leafing through a magazine and they will, for the most part, start at the back, or part-way through, and work to the front. In the process, the page which catches their eye most frequently is the right-hand page. Moreover, the format of magazines and newspapers is such that even when opened in what might be thought of as the conventional way, by those who do not conform to the aforesaid general rule, the first page revealed to the gaze is the right-hand one. And in practically every case where the right-hand page is observed first, it is almost always the top right-hand corner that is focused upon.

Ask me why this should be so and I will rapidly change the subject. No doubt some behavioural psychologist somewhere has the answer; but don't let's ask otherwise we shall be here all night. It's sufficient, I think, to say that it does happen; and sufficient evidence to try, wherever possible, to position ads at the top right-hand corner of a right-hand page. In newspapers, the premium page is said to be page three. I leave you to make anything of that you so wish.

There's a snag, of course. There always is when you latch on to something beneficial – isn't that right? In this instance, the snag is that you will have to pay more to gain the advantage of a 'special position'.

Other special positions in this category are: front-page

solus (or any solus) – which, as its name implies, is an ad that sits alone amid editorial, and which is generally of a specified size; ear spaces (title corners); any space on a particular feature page – motoring, gardening, women's page, etc.; and anywhere else you *particularly* request.

I should also tell you that special positions are much sought after by advertisers and are often booked up for months in advance. In fact, the availability of special positions reduces in direct proportion to your eagerness to secure them. This shall henceforth be known as Quinn's second law of thwart. The first law, should you be interested, says: in any given pub, being first in line at the bar guarantees that the barman will go and check the cellar.

But none of this should stop you from trying for special positions should you need them.

The alternative is to buy your space run-of-paper (ROP). This means appearing anywhere the publication's make-up people care to place you. Yet ROP has the advantage of costing less. Like they say, money talks. You pay it and you take your choice.

If pressed, I would say that it pays to blow the extra cash and buy into special positions – but with one notable exception. Magazine front covers.

There is a practically universal custom among industrial and technical publications to turn their front covers over to advertisers. It is, I have no doubt, a first-class method of generating revenue, since these pages cannot be bought for shirt-buttons. However, I beg to doubt their usefulness to the advertiser as a promotional medium; and my doubts are strongly held.

I suppose I look at more trade magazines than most people. And the first thing I notice about them is the front cover. Or, more often than not, it's the first thing I don't notice. One tends, I believe, to look at the front cover as a front cover rather than as an advertisement; and it occurs to me that if this mental attitude is as general to others as it is as peculiar to me, then this position may not be as 'special' as it is cracked up to be.

Certainly these positions are special; certainly they are

dominating; certainly they almost always offer scope for colour, or equally dramatic work; and certainly they are expensive. But are they looked at? Are they noticed? Or are they largely glanced at and turned over unassimilated? I have a feeling that the question which rates the most frequent 'yes' is the third.

Maybe there has been some solid research done on the impact and readership of front covers of technical journals. If so, I should be interested to hear of its findings – preparatory to disbelieving them. But until someone overwhelms me with a whole pile of indisputable figures, I shall continue to harbour doubts as to their effectiveness, pound for pound, as against inside positions.

We'll leave it there, shall we?

Now let's take a look at what you'll put, physically speaking, into the spaces you have booked.

★ ★ ★

For reasons quite beyond my understanding, the printing trade has an aura of mystery about it which seems to be absent in most other trades. This is possibly because you can't buy a composing stick or a case of type in your local DIY shop the way you can buy the tools of the plumbing, carpentry and building trades. On the other hand, it may be that printers are more than usually anxious to protect their craft from the encroachment of louts off the street who fancy their chances.

As someone who has served time in the composing room (though no less a lout for all that), I can tell you that there was once a period when printing required a high degree of manual dexterity and a straight eye. Compliments of the microchip, however, this is, in the main, no longer true. Whether it is better off for it, I reserve my right to stay silent.

These days, typesetting is done to an ever-increasing degree on word processors of a certain sort; and the whole business is considerably cleaner.

The result of all this is that today's compositor is a cross between a copytypist and a paste-up artist. What it also means is that any of the aforementioned louts who are able to use a typewriter, rub down the odd word in Letraset, and rule a straight line can produce their own artwork. For ads; for leaflets; for stationery.

What exactly is artwork? Without wishing to insult your intelligence, any piece of typed, hand-drawn or printed material – as long as it is in black-and-white, clean and sharply defined – can be used as artwork. All you have to do is paste down the item to be reproduced on to a piece of artboard and the printer will do the rest. What he does, in fact, is photograph the item, make a negative and, from that, produce a printing plate.

Thus, to make artwork for a complete ad, you merely require the ingredients of, say, typeset or Letraset headline; typeset or typed body copy; an illustration where necessary; a copy of your logo; and address details, again typeset or typed. These separate pieces are then positioned according to taste within your ad framework and stuck down. So when your printer asks for camera-ready artwork, this is what he means.

You can buy typesetting to order, and to your copy details, from any of hundreds of specialist typesetting houses around the country. You can trace your local outfit through the *Yellow Pages*.

Do-it-yourself artwork can be done by the amateur – and very successfully, too – provided he or she has a feel for design and an eye for graphic balance. It will also pay to immerse yourself in a book or two on the subject of typefaces. What also helps is access to a reducing/enlarging photocopier, since it is far easier to make artwork once or twice up on the finished size and then reduce it in proportion.

Modern electronic typewriters are a god-send to the do-it-yourselfer. Those which employ proportional spacing, which 'justify' lines so that each is printed to exactly the same length, and which provide a variety of typestyles (some of them almost indistinguishable from regular faces), are nothing short of modern miracles.

But I emphasize that the quality of the print must be crystal clear and razor-sharp; and the paper you use should be a smooth matt with no lumpy bits or fibres. Spend a couple of quid in your local art shop on 'repro' paper and get it absolutely right.

Type plays an important part in ad layout, of course. Meaning that your choice of typeface can make or break the ad. Faces, particularly those used in headlines, should reflect the message you are attempting to put across.

Take, for instance, a florist wishing to promote the idea of a gift of flowers on Mother's Day. He would be most unwise to employ a bold, chunky type with huge serifs hanging from it. (Serifs are the short lines at right angles to the tops and bottoms of letter strokes.) His message would be much more acceptable in a slim, delicate and appropriately feminine typeface.

The converse would be true of the promotion of, say, excavating machinery in an industrial publication. Big and powerful those machines are – so big and powerful should be the look of the typeface.

These are fairly extreme examples; though no matter what business you are in there's a typeface to suit you. Whatever you do, though, stay away from Old English faces and 'fun faces'. Old English is a popular face with funeral directors for their letterheads and tariffs and such. The fun faces referred to are those which have: (a) shadow effects; (b) oddly shaped letters; (c) reversed out lettering, i.e. letters which appear as white on black; and (d) busy filigree swarming all over them. These are fine as headlines to magazine editorials. They are worse than useless in ads – for the reason that they are difficult to read – and people won't even attempt to read an ad that doesn't give up its secrets on the instant.

Next, illustration. The rule here is if you have nothing to illustrate (and I mean nothing), don't feel compelled to include a picture simply for the sake of it. A well designed all-type ad can be extremely powerful. Much more so than one which consists of a printer's stock-block (a standard illustration) as the focal point and a sales message laid out

willy-nilly around it. Moreover, printers' stock-blocks
have usually been around in composing room cases for
many years. These get resurrected from time to time, with
little thought for whom they were last used. So that super
line illustration of a dicky-bowed waiter promoting your
exclusive restaurant could well have appeared a fortnight
ago in an ad for the local repertory company's production of
The Butler Did It!

To get a look at a comprehensive range of typefaces, pick
up a Letraset catalogue at any good art shop. Incidentally,
Letraset not only produce sheets of faces that can, with a
little practice, be laid down quite expertly and be made to
look like pukka typesetting, but also supply a variety of
tints, patterns, symbols, and architectural and general
illustrations. I would say, without much fear of contra-
diction that the average design studio would come to an
abrupt halt if Letraset ever decided to give up business.

I don't advocate that everyone should do their own
artwork, neither do I recommend it as a matter of principle,
because not everyone has the patience nor, to be brutally
frank, the ability. But I think everyone should certainly
give it a try. And if you can draw and use a camera, that's a
bonus. Yet everything you do should be more than
comparable with professionally made ads – and be able to sit
unselfconsciously among them. One of the greatest faults
with any home-grown photography can usually be seen in
the lighting technique employed by the cameraman; and the
major problem with amateur illustrating is the rigidity of
composition and the lack of fluidity in the style.

Lighting a product shot is not easy. I have witnessed
professional camermen spending whole days setting up
shots, and still being far from delirious with the result. My
simple advice, if you are hoping to produce your own
photography, is to do more than read a book on the subject.
Go one better and ask a friendly photographer to allow you
to sit in on one of his jobs. And I mean an advertising
photographer, not one of those fellows who spends his
weekends recording weddings.

Illustrating isn't a doddle either. Examine the cartoons in

this book. They are simple one-liners which, it might be thought, anyone can produce. Not so. A slickness the like of this isn't such as you can pull out of a Christmas cracker. Nevertheless, you should have a go – at everything.

But when in doubt, leave it to the professionals. You will have to pay, of course; and there's no way around that. However, if you take note of what I'm about to say, you ought not pay so much.

★　　★　　★

Given that you prefer not to do it yourself, you can leave the preparation of your ads to the publication in which you aim to appear, and leave the design of printed material to any decent printer. For a more personal, and possibly more committed approach to your work, hire yourself an artist.

Here are the drawbacks. In the first two instances, you will be buying the services of people who know everything there is to know about the mechanics of printing, but who very likely have no formal print-design training. Any design skills as they may possess will have been picked up rather more by accident than intention. I'm aware that some of the larger newspapers and print-shops employ designers in-house, but these are not in the majority. In the printer's favour is the fact that the cost of designing your work will be laid off against, or lost within, the price of the print-job itself. Similarly, in the case of papers and magazines, design and setting charges are all-inclusive in the price of the space booked – they will comp your ads free of charge.

I hope printers will understand when I say that much printer-designed work is not as exciting as it might be. They may even feel tempted to agree with me. Though when I go one step farther and declare that the large volume of it is dull, old-fashioned and unexceptional, I am probably risking a swift and uncompromising raspberry. Nevertheless, I believe it to be true; and I believe it to the extent that I would think twice before asking a printer to design my work.

The advertising artist, on the other hand, will be

someone who has almost certainly had training in the techniques of visualizing, design and finished art. This being so, it follows that he or she will also have a foot planted firmly in the door of modern design trends, and will know the quickest and cheapest way of achieving the effects you are aiming for.

But how do you locate and tame an artist? More to the point, how do you find an artist who has a greater interest in the standard of the work he produces than in the money he is paid to do it? The answer to both these questions is a resounding: easily.

Creative people are, on the whole, ingenuous people. By the very nature of their work – which is motivated by the proportions of half commercial necessity and half creative urge – they tend to view life as a less than serious affair, and money as an unavoidable evil. Consequently, there are few rich artists; not because they don't deserve to be rich, but because they are inclined not to seek riches. It is for these reasons that they are often taken to the financial cleaners by people who are less moved to play fair than you are or I am. And also the reason why they are largely prepared to take on a low-pay exercise simply for the joy of turning out 'decent work'. More so, as it happens, than any other profession I can think of – apart, maybe, from copywriters. Can you just see a plumber operating to a similar philosophy? 'Yes, missus, I'll fit your bathroom suite for half the normal charge, on account of its such a lovely colour.'

Neither can I. And I'm not knocking plumbers; rather, I'm faulting creative people for their unworldly stance.

Anyway, the following procedure for locating a designer will work just as well for copywriters, photographers, and any other freelance service you may need. So, first, walk through the *Yellow Pages* and call every graphic design outfit in your locality. Tell them, in no uncertain terms, that you are a small firm with not a lot to spend. Then tell them exactly how much is in your advertising/promotions budget, along with the codicil that you will not be disbursing more than 20 per cent of the total sum on press and print production. Like this you are making it plain that initial design concepts, artwork and illustration for ads and other promotional stuff (mailers, leaflets, brochures, even letterheads, etc.) must come to no more than the going rate. Unless you ratify this basic ground-rule, they will take the bit between their teeth and produce work beyond your purse; and you will live to see your entire budget swallowed up on a bundle of mechanical material that you cannot afford to put into production.

Putting the remainder of the figures together, you spend the 80 per cent balance on advertising space and on actual printing of mailers, or whatever.

Always set a limit for creative people above which they cannot go. Always.

Unlike most tradesmen, who can give you a hard-and-fast quote for a piece of work, the designer or writer has no precise mathematical formula by which to assess how long a job will take. Being creative, they require thinking time; and being perfectionists, they won't want to sacrifice looks and accuracy in favour of speed.

At any rate, your telephone call and 20 per cent limit will bring one of three responses. We shall discuss only two of them since the third is too impolite for rendering in so genteel a publication as this one.

1 An offer to take on your work, subject to the proviso that should your requirements call for greater production time/cost, they will say so in advance.
2 An affable 'no thanks' with, if you press it, a recommendation to get in touch with a hungry freelance of their acquaintance, who might be prepared to handle your work on your terms.

Another way of finding the necessary people is to call the ad agencies in your area. Speak to the creative director in each case.

It so happens that agencies employ freelances from time to time. More often, in truth, than agencies would care to admit, seeing as how they sell themselves to their clients as 'full service' agencies, i.e. with everything under one roof and on tap.

Remarkably, the response you get from the agency will be more than cordial. Well, they don't want to handle your account – it would be more trouble to them than it is worth; but in pointing you in the direction of freelance sources, they will be doing both you and themselves a favour. This patronage, as it were, is essentially pragmatic. The freelance in question will be delighted at the recommendation and will, thereafter, be prepared to turn somersaults for the agency in order to repay the goodwill.

A final method of unearthing a designer or writer, is via a publication called *The Creative Handbook*. This annual lists hundreds of freelance people around the country, and it can be got direct from Creative Handbook, 100 St Martin's Lane, London WC2N 4AZ. (Telephone: 01 379 7399.)

Once you've located the freelance, you will need to come to a sound working arrangement. The going rate for a good designer or writer is around £30 to £40 an hour – about the same as you'd pay for a good solicitor. This, and more, is what they charge agencies; but if you establish an overall price for the job beforehand, there can be no argument.

I have always considered this hourly rate lark to be a bit of a con. After all, different people work at different speeds; so who's to prove or, indeed, disprove, how long a particular piece of work took? Most of the time, too, the writer and designer can operate a damn sight faster than the uninitiated would credit.

An ex-client of mine, and I emphasize the ex, recently got himself into a jam by booking time at a radio studio in which he was hoping to produce a commercial that he had written. Problem was, *his* client overnight turned down the proposed script root and branch; and it looked very much as if my chap was stuck with paying a studio-cancellation fee. To get himself out of trouble, what he needed was a new script.

Call for Pat Quinn.

It was 8.35 a.m. 'I'm in the studio at ten. Can you do me a thirty-second script to the following brief? I'll come round and pick it up now, and then get it approved by the client before going into the studio.'

I had the thing written and typed in less than fifteen minutes. It was ready and waiting when he came in. He read it briefly, nodded approvingly, then said as bold as brass: 'Seeing as how this only took you a few minutes, you won't be charging for it – will you?'

Hence, ex-client.

The way I evaluate the worth of a job is like this. The man who uses only one nail to mend your fence, doesn't get paid according to the cost of the nail. He gets paid for knowing exactly where to put it. Thus, if you find a good freelance who makes his job look childishly simple, don't take that as a cue to cut his wages. Similarly, if you find one who is prepared to work for less than the going rate, treat him or her with respect and go out of your way to praise their efforts. Don't nit-pick; and don't, unless the job is miles off the marketing target, get into senseless arguments about style or treatment.

A writer or designer, if he is any good, knows he is risking his reputation every time one of his ads appears in the papers. In this respect, he has as much to lose, if the work is bad, as you do. Also, if he is any good, he will believe that he can do his job far better than you can do his job. And 99 per cent of the time, he will be right. So let him do it.

Within the constraints of the budget, give him his head. Latch on to him. Get alongside him. Don't expect him to *want* to keep coming to your factory, shop or office. He won't. But drag him along and involve him. Writers and designers don't like meeting clients any more than clients like meeting them; but swallow your natural antipathy for people who do business wearing scruffy jeans and ancient sneakers, and meet him more than halfway. Tell him *everything* you know about whatever it is you make or do. Tell him your plans and your hopes; your dreams and ambitions. Involve him in every aspect of your business. Don't expect him to know right away as much about it as you do; and don't expect him to learn it in five minutes. Teach him. Enthuse him.

Do this, and your writer or designer won't care tuppence if all you are spending is tuppence.

To put it shorter, you want someone who isn't afraid to say 'no' when they consider 'yes' to be the wrong answer. You want someone who, while casting wistful glances at full-colour pages in *The Sunday Times* supplement, can still do a first-class job with a 20 cm double column in monochrome in the *Ballsover Bugle*.

To put it shorter still, you want a designer or a writer you can get along with. Because arguing with people you like (and you'll have to argue from time to time), is easier than arguing with people you don't. And once you've found him or her, take pains to keep them.

★　★　★

Wherever possible, use only one designer or writer for all your work. Don't chop and change as the whim takes you, or in the mistaken belief that it will act *pour encourager les autre*. It won't. All it will serve to do is switch them off. Stick to one bloke or lady to produce designs for your office stationery and vehicle livery, as well as your advertising and sales literature. That way, there will be seen to be a definable pattern; a corporate identity or strategy from the brain of one person, rather than the rag-bag of diverse ideas you are likely to get if you employ different people at different times.

So now you have your freelance. Ok – sit them down and pose some questions like: 'What can we do for this much money?' And: 'What do *you* think we should do for this much money?' Plus some statements along these lines: 'If what you are suggesting works to the extent where my sales are increased by more than X%, I'll give you a bonus of £Y.'

You will, I assure you, be mightily impressed by the effort which will be put in on your behalf after such pledges. More, much more, than the money you are paying warrants, I'll bet.

★　★　★

While I'm on the subject of money, please bear with me while I make a point about the cost of advertising production – in a mechanical sense, that is.

It will, I think, not arouse a great deal of controversy, if I say that industrial/retail advertisers as a species, are not particularly renowned for the lavishness of their spending on the production of their advertisements. Indeed, I will go so far as to opine that the average advertising manager reacts to any given invoice in much the same way as Superman does to green Kryptonite.

This accounts, understandably up to a point, for the continued and boring incidence of stock photographs and illustrations of such items as pill bottles, supermarket trolleys, fork-lift trucks, unlabelled food tins and similar but uninspiring artifacts. (Stock shots, as you may know, are standard library pictures specific to nobody and general to all, and may be used, on payment of a small hire fee, by anyone. Certainly the fee is smaller than what it might cost to professionally originate them.) They appear with the inevitability of death and taxes, in any randomly chosen issue of any randomly chosen trade journal; and while to their makers they may be a joy forever, few of them can reasonably be described as things of beauty. The trouble with most of them is that they make wearisome ads; and paying out good money to weary people has never seemed to me to be anything like a sensible proposition.

Therefore, I feel constrained to suggest, in the passing, that it might be a sound idea for anyone who is charged with the disposal of a few hard-wrung advertising pounds to consider this: that to cut your space expenditure by a little; and thereby to increase your production expenditure by (relatively) a lot, might not be as heretical as it may seem.

Keeping the maximum frequency of ad insertion is, and I should be the last to deny it, a most commendable aim. But I leave you with this thought: if you are in the habit of spending, say, £4,000 on space for ten dreary ads that no one notices, might it not be better to spend £1,000 on producing an ad that people *will* notice and to run it only seven times.

(A note for the mathematically minded. If you can think

of nothing positive to do with the spare £200, allow me to recommend a charity close to my heart. It is the Society for Indigent Copywriters, of which I am the chairman and sole member.)

Stock-shots and stock illustrations look exactly what they are: general purpose instruments; and when you see the same ones periodically aired for a variety of different products, their weakness is exposed. So whenever you need to include pictures in ads, include your own, home-grown efforts. And wherever you can, put a touch more money into your production effort.

I understand that this counsel, if taken as seriously as it should be, could drive half the photo-libraries in Britain swiftly to the wall. In which case, I only hope that you, sir or madam, are not in the stock-picture business in any serious way.

I really do.

6 Getting publicity

Getting publicity, whether it's for yourself or for somebody else, isn't all that difficult. In fact, it's not difficult at all.

To make the headlines, all you have to do is go out and banjo a well-known politician (you'll know the one I mean) and the rest will be taken care of for you.

A little more enigmatical, however, is the achievement of publicity – the realization of effective communications – in support of a business objective.

So tell us something we don't already know, you say. And tell us something else, if you will. If you are so all-fired marvellous at this advertising/publicity business, how come we've never heard of you?

Good question; and one I'll answer like this: nobody pays me to publicize myself. But over the years, I have been paid to publicize other people. Other people like Dunlop, Whyte & Mackay, Alfa Romeo, Kwik-Fit, Kerrygold, Stanley Tools and Canon. I guess you've heard of *them*?

The object of public relations, then, is to create a favourable climate in which a business can operate. In other words, the idea is to build a credit balance of goodwill between your firm and the public at large. This is achieved by disseminating information about the company via press, radio, TV, newsletters and, of course, word of mouth – to anyone who wants to know it.

Well, great, you chime. Great if you've got an awful lot of time to spend on preparing such things. Not to mention cash. In any case, we're only a piddling little concern in whom nobody has anything like a deep and abiding interest. The punters buy our merchandise once every so often, and forget all about us in between times.

But do they? And if they do – why do they? What exactly happens in that period between purchases? Who do your customers talk to and, more significantly, listen to? How many other piddling little firms (or even piddling big ones) hammer endlessly upon their doors in the hope of pulling the business that you accept as a matter of course?

The general public is nothing if not fickle. And it is becoming fickler by the minute. Therefore, for you to rely upon past services rendered as the means of guaranteeing future services unrendered is, to say the least of it, wishful thinking. It's about as bright as banking on Lucky Lad in the 3.30 to be the provider of next month's mortgage – and just about as doomed.

At this very moment, yes, your customers may be thoroughly delighted with your goods and services; yet come tomorrow, for whatever reason, they could go right off the boil. You may be familiar with the old adage which runs: 'You can do them nine favours on the trot, but if you fail to do the tenth you are a self-centred swine!'

I suspect this quaint aphorism was coined by one of those small business people who had no time for public relations – who thought that as long as he turned out the product, people would continue to pay him money for it – just as he went into liquidation.

Did I, a moment ago, say that the public is fickle? Perhaps 'more aware' might be a better way of putting it. These days, people have more choice than they've ever had; and the power they wield with that choice can bring even the largest of organizations whimpering to heel. They use that power of choice, too, by demanding even more for their money. More services – more servicing. And what's more, they get it.

I'm not saying that, as a nation, we are becoming more selfish (or maybe I am); but what we are doing – and pretty rapidly, by the way – is changing out attitudes to other people in general and to companies in particular. For whatever reasons, we are becoming a 'now' society. Not in the sense of a modern, go-getting, all-vogue society, but rather an I-want-it-now society.

So no matter how reliable, honest, courteous, dedicated, decent or responsive our present supplier may be, we are constantly goading ourselves into the pursuit of a more reliable, honest, courteous, dedicated, etc. supplier to do our bidding.

I reckon part of the malaise, if that's what it is, arises as a direct result of all those dreadful consumer-watchdog newspaper columns and TV programmes one sees betimes. They purport to unmask large-scale fraudsters, but for the most part only succeed in exposing tatty little crooks who make the green-goods men and bunco artists of the 1920s look like Raffles. I'm afraid the really big-time consumer crooks can only be stopped by an Act of Parliament. But that is another axe, and this is the wrong grindstone – so I'll say no more.

Essentially, all of this awareness, choice and 'help and advice' (which is something else you have thrust under your nose every time you switch on the television) has made it necessary even for small businesses to go public from time to time, in order to keep their customers *au fait*. Small businesses, because they *are* small, are vulnerable to public attitudes. Mistrust is the norm, and they are often viewed as shoestring organizations controlled by fly-by-nights.

Anything you can do, therefore, to assuage these doubts and eliminate uncalled for attitudes, can only be good. More so when, by and large, it happens to be free.

★   ★   ★

I have no ambition to pull any wool over your eyes. I will say, then, right at the outset, that any items of information you may care to prepare about your company will not see themselves published purely as a matter of course. PR material is as subject to the freakishnesses of chance – or, rather, the whims of the publication editorial-staff involved – as anything ever was. Moreover, I shall not pontificate about what you should do, without showing you how you should do it. (I hope I have already proved that I am not another of those writers who possibly show how very easy

it is to have an idea, without ever requiring to have one.)
Later on we *shall* do it.

The most fertile ground for PR exploitation is to be
found in regional newspapers, and regional radio and
television. These 'locals' thrive on news for, of and about
people, clubs, companies and organizations operating in
their area. And the reason for their continued success is
clear. Readers, listeners and viewers enjoy seeing their own
doings, and the doings of their neighbours promulgated in
the media – especially if, in the latter case, these happen to
be dirty doings; and the popularity of the medium in
question is in direct proportion to its insularity.

It is true to say that remarkably little news is handed to
the media by the general public. Much of it comes from
news agencies, but the largest proportion is the result of
able journalism: the result of prying, probing and good,
old-fashioned leg-work. Thus, anyone who can gain the
confidence of a local journalist by presenting him with a
useable story every now and then, will be seen as a reliable
source of information.

This is exactly what those mohair-suited, digital-
watched PR executives are overpaid to do.

All of the above, of course, holds likewise for the news-
gathering side of trade and technical publications. Allowing
that you specialize in a business or trade (and when you
think about it, everyone specializes in something), if the
news you offer has substance, you may quickly become a
quotable authority. In this joyful circumstance, when you
are approached to give your considered opinion on a
particular situation, don't speculate – especially if it's a crisis
situation. By all means hand down a judgement based on
the facts as you know them, but never theorize.

What is news? A newsworthy story is one that contains
elements that are, from a moral point of view, either very
good, very bad, or downright ugly. But what, in specific
terms, will the media consider a worthwhile proposition
for inclusion in their pages or programmes?

Here are twelve, tried-and-tested gambits for a printable
story:

1 *The launching of a new product* – particularly if it has a social value. Like, for instance, a new kind of public litter-basket, several of which may be offered to the local authority free of charge, for use in the district's memorial gardens, say.

2 *An interesting new customer*; a titled person or a popular personality who buys duvets/tyres/insurance from you. (This can only be done with the express permission of the personality, however.)

3 *How you went to great lengths to help a customer.* You hired a helicopter/private plane to fly a badly-needed part for an excavator to an outlandish site in the Highlands. The trip cost £400, the part was worth only £15, but you kept a good customer.

   Or, again, you completely re-wired a pensioner's home absolutely free when you discovered – while installing a simple plug-point – that the wiring was hazardous.

4 *The personal achievement of one of your employees.* He, or she, has won a Duke of Edinburgh Gold Award; has been given a place at the Royal Academy of Music; or has collected £3,000 for charity. Don't forget to mention that you gave said employee encouragement and time off to pursue these activities – if, in fact, you did.

5 *Sponsorship.* Your own sponsorship of a local drama group, Formula Ford racing driver, football team, or festival.

6 *The numbers racket.* You have just made your millionth Christmas tree stand, or served your umpteenth customer.

7 *An organized 'stunt'* which has a logical connection with your business, product or service. For example, the hiring of a military band to help promote the launch of the new *Adjutant* car at your showroom.

8 *The appointment of a new director*, sales manager, etc. – especially if he or she is known locally.

9 *Announcing future plans*; diversifying into another area of business; or the purchase of newer, bigger, historic premises.

10   *Employment.* You have taken on X new employees to
      help satisfy increased demand for your product. You
      also envisage taking on more people in the near future.
11   *An open day* at your factory or showroom. Or a shop-
      window unusually dressed to mark a historic local
      event or national anniversary.
12   *A grand opening* by a personality.

There are dozens more newsworthy ideas to dream up
once you get your mind working. But whatever story you
decide to release, don't release it exclusively to the media.
There's no harm whatever in giving it direct to your
customers and potential customers, as well. So include
them on the mailing list.

Good PR requires a clarity of purpose in what you hope
to achieve. So, first, substantiate the problem or subject on
which you wish to communicate.

Is your organization about to launch a new product? If it
is, who should be informed? And what will their interest
be? Again, is your company experiencing a 'bad press', or
being affected by malicious rumour arising out of some
unfortunate incident with a customer? Or by tales of
bankruptcy? In which case, will a public announcement
ease the tension? And, further, has your market-research
shown that only a fraction of the people canvassed has any
clear idea of the full extent of your services and activities?
That being so, what will it take to put the full story across?

Once you know what PR action is necessary, the
audience will identify itself.

Generally speaking, you are attempting to plant an image
of your firm in the minds of others. Never confuse image
with identity. Image, in these terms, is the impression that
others have of you. Identity is your uniqueness, your way
of doing things – it's even the typeface you use on your
letterheads and the colours you choose to paint your vans.

The next stage in the process is the selection of your
various audiences, or 'publics'. Define them with care; they
could be customers, potential customers, the public at
large, even your own employees. The latter is most

important; your employees need to know what you're doing, and where you're going, as much as anybody.

All you have to do now is contact the selected public via the press and broadcasting media, as mentioned, and via mailing shots direct.

I don't have to tell you that this is easier said than done. So let's figure out how it can be done.

★ ★ ★

Lay your hands on a publication called *Hollis Press & Public Relations Annual*, and another titled *Benn's Press Directory*. Between them, these two volumes will give you the addresses and contact-names of just about every professional, vocational and consumer organization, and every newspaper, magazine and broadcasting service in the UK. From them, you can glean the point of contact for your press releases, and draw up a mailing of likely users of your material.

On the trade-magazine front, canvass editors to put your new product on the test-bench page; and have them air their considered opinion of it. The chances of them doing so, unless you take a certain amount of advertising space in their publications, are not good. But you could always try the old ploy of promising to take space at some later date – *if* their analysis of your product first creates enough market interest to make the spending of money a viable proposition. You will almost certainly be obliged to compromise on this issue. Editors aren't daft and they've heard all the promises well before today. Yet no editor will turn you down flat if it transpires that your product has readership mileage. After all, magazines sell on the basis of their content; so the featuring of a bright new invention, or a clever slant on an existing theme, will be seen as a plum story by the editorial staff and a scoop by the readers. In which case you'll get a review with no strings.

Now for the format of the press release. In formulating the release, bear in mind that you are trying to communicate as rapidly as possible with some amazingly busy people. They have no time to read acres of flowery prose; they want to be able to pick out the gist of your story in seconds rather than minutes, and anything which appears even mildly wordy will be bucketed without too much ceremony. Presentation must be short, sharp and very much to the point. Contain everything you want to say on one page – in fact, hold it down to 150 words or less; and have it accurately and neatly typed with double-line spacing. Where a piece has promise, the subeditor will either run it as it stands, or put a blue pencil through it to bring it down to the proportions he requires. Should it be an item of outstanding merit, you can bank on it that he will contact you double-quick for any further embellishment.

On the length issue, therefore, short is far more acceptable than long.

Most of the companies which go in for PR in any substantial way, invariably have a special letterhead suitably overprinted with the legend *Press Release*. This is generally in red. At the very least it looks professional, at the most it will declare exactly what you're offering; and if it helps to bring your stuff a more than cursory glance, it must be worthwhile.

What about the story proper? Initially, we must write a headline – one that reveals the plot at a glance. No need to be clever, here. Plays on words and puns are, first and foremost, uncalled for and, in the final analysis, stand a good chance of being misunderstood.

Next, we desire an opening sentence that gives a precise and factual summary of the full story. This should be as concise as possible and contain the minimum of subclauses. The remaining blurb will then reinforce both the headline and the 'opener' with hard facts.

Perhaps we should write a release, here and now, so as to give you a better picture of the structure.

All right, imagine if you will the simple proposition that our small, Birmingham-based plastics company – Clearview Mouldings Ltd – has landed a contract to supply the Ministry of Agriculture with 20,000 plant-propagators for use in their experimental research nurseries at Tiveton. The deal is worth £1,000,000, which revenue will almost double our turnover this year; and the contract was won in the face of stiff opposition from rival companies. To satisfy the contract, it looks as though we shall be obliged to hire a couple of new employees.

That's the plot; while the audience is anybody and everybody, since we are simply telling the world that our little firm is capable of big things. How about the headline? Something like this, maybe:

MIDLANDS FIRM IN £1,000,000 GOVERNMENT DEAL

Or, perhaps:

£1,000,000 MINISTRY CONTRACT FOR BIRMINGHAM PLASTICS COMPANY

Both inordinately simple; both direct and to the point. The opening paragraph, then, would run along these lines:

Clearview Mouldings Limited, the Birmingham-based plastics company, has clinched a £1M contract with the Ministry of Agriculture.

And so into the facts of the matter:

The contract, which is to supply 20,000 plant propagators for the Ministry's experimental research nurseries in Tiverton, Devon, was won in competition with a number of other firms.

Managing director, Manuel Labour, describes the deal as a shot in the arm for his company – which currently employs less than a dozen workers. 'This will open a lot of doors for us; and we are looking seriously at plant-expansion and a recruitment programme. Our first step will be to take on a number of extra employees.'

Which is about all that's necessary, apart from:

For further information, please contact:
Burlington R. Cade (Sales Manager)
(Telephone)

Remember, of course, to date it.

You may hold that the piece is altogether too short for your taste and might be strengthened by the addition of the odd bit of company background. Well, just so long as you don't tear the fundament out of it, otherwise you'll never get published.

A general word now about copy deadlines. Daily papers and broadcasting news departments work to an immediacy that makes 'now' seem positively archaic. It will be wholly prudent, therefore, if your story has a limited life, to phone the respective news editors and transmit the bones of it there and then. Should the piece be of interest to them, they'll either transfer you to a reporter, or send one round to see you.

Before you do that, however, think the thing through, on several counts. First, be certain that your story is newsworthy. Don't cry wolf, don't try to push stories which patently have no backbone; because when the time comes that you do have a really spanking item, you'll be disregarded. Second, work out in your mind (or on paper) exactly what it is you want to tell the editor. And, above all, be enthusiastic. Enthusiasm, like measles, is highly contagious.

Trade magazines, on the other hand, work to longer lead times. But this in itself can present problems. On a monthly publication, as an example, most of the material is put to bed many weeks before the publication date; and the editorial staff works at least a month, sometimes several months, in advance. This, in turn, means, that you will be wise to think well ahead about any launch or promotion which might have news value. In such circumstances, send out a pre-launch, 'introductory' release marked: *Not for publication until such and such a date*, then send a post-launch summary.

I said previously that the nature of the story will predict the media most suitable for the release. The story example given above would very probably find a home in the locals and nationals (press and broadcasting), as well as the plastics' trade press. However, had the contract been for a foreign government, we should also have released to the various news agencies and the Central Office of Information – which represent invaluable channels for the outlet of this type of material. Similarly, a general interest piece which announced an event taking place at some time in the future, would have gone to the BBC's Future Events Unit.

Any photographs you may care to send along with a release will certainly assist your cause. Though these should be excellent black-and-white shots, no less than 200 × 75 mm (8 × 5 in) and preferably taken by a professional. Don't shoot in colour without first confirming that the publication will take it. Monochrome prints *can* be made from colour work, but the process always results in a loss of definition.

Bland shots of factory exteriors are not very exciting, and not much use unless you are in the factory-building business. Aerial pictures are likewise dreary, except where you need to prove a point about location. Product pictures should have life and sparkle – this all comes down, as we've said, to lighting and composition. So it's worth spending a little extra money to have somebody do it right. After all, with any luck your product will be around for a long time. In which case you might as well put together a photographic portfolio which will last equally as long.

Product shots aside, where it's feasible get people into the picture; and I will own that pictures made solely for PR purposes are the one area where I would countenance the use of a *soupçon* of female pulchritude. Although I wouldn't make it mandatory, I would certainly not rule it out.

★   ★   ★

I apologize in advance if the following section is liable to be something of a dog's dinner; but even a dog has to eat some time.

There are two reasons for this. The first is that there are numerous bits and pieces which I have been meaning to comment on and which it is high time I got round to. The second is that what I have to discuss is not pure PR, but rather publicity generally.

Let's kick off with 'identity'. We have already seen that a company's identity is its special way of going about things – the face it presents to the world. From this comes its image, or the view that others have of it. Thus, if a firm's identity is a hotch-potch of unco-ordinated, unrelated ideas, then the impression it leaves people with will be similarly messy.

The first place to begin examining a company's identity is in its name. So that's where we shall start.

What's in a name? Just about everything, I would say. An engineering firm called Precision Works will present a far more positive face, and have a damned sight more chance of succeeding than one calling itself A & B Engineering. Equally, a hairdressing salon going under a title like Scissors, say, ought to be somewhat more sought after than one called Bert's Barbers. These are pretty extreme examples, yet they happen to exist.

Also very relevant to achieving sales is what you decide to call a product.

It's a sad reflection of our society that the traditional butcher is going swiftly down the Swanee, and is being ousted by the far less personal – and decidedly impersonal – supermarket shelf. Why? Because the young meat-buying market is so uneducated in the science of meat-cuts that it becomes embarrassed when confronted by a real butcher, who might stoop to enquire whether the steak as asked for is for stewing or frying. Young shoppers find it much simpler, much less harrowing, to snatch their pre-packed selection from a freezer cabinet. No questions asked, no decisions to be made in public. As much as people may profess to yearn for the return of the old-style shopkeeper, they mostly elect for the anonymity and quickness of the superstore.

Given this to be the ghastly truth that it is, there is no wonder that the major manufacturers spend hundreds of thousands on devising and researching product names. Rightly, they have no wish to alienate three parts of their market by presenting a product with a name which might be difficult to pronounce, or distressing to utter. Hence, product names are, for the most part, elementary in construction; are usually representative of what the product is; and are calculated not to put anyone into a state of anguish should they feel compelled to speak them.

Some years ago, I had the job of contriving a name for a new brand of dog food (well, someone has to do it). This substance was reputed to contain the customary ingredients of wholesome meat, wheat-meal, added vitamins, plus, wait for it, egg. At the time, the addition of egg was thought in some quarters to be something of a culinary masterstroke; and it was predicted that the stuff would move like curry through a goose. The product name, therefore, had to be symbolic of egg and somehow emotive of dog.

My own dog, a Border collie called Bonzo, took one look at the sample bowlful I offered, growled, lowered his ears and strolled away. Our cat, an otherwise voracious tabby known as Korky, also declined to have anything to do with it. (This has very little bearing on the story, but it may help to get me some work on the editorial staff of the *Beano*.)

After much backwarding and forwarding, the name the client chose from my long list – and the one I had included for amusement rather than serious consideration – was *Ouef*! Which, you must surely agree, is representative of egg and redolent of the canine utterance. But it was hardly likely to have people streaming into dog-food shops and barking for it by name. Once he had chosen it, however, he could not be talked out of it – despite my very best efforts. And that goes to show that if you are bent on being stupid, you may as well make a thorough and studied job of it.

Luckily for everyone concerned, the product never went into production.

I think this indicates pretty graphically that the choice of a product name is just about as important as the product itself. Really, it all depends on who it is you are selling to.

Kids don't mind asking for Curly-Wurlys and Wham-Bammers, but insist that a grown man does the same and there is a likelihood that he will tell you where to shove it. By the same principle, a woman wouldn't think twice about requesting a perfume called Sensual, but might baulk at asking for a deodorant named Randy.

So name it according to the proclivities of the person who might buy it.

There is a confusing propensity among many industrial firms to give their products both a name and a number. Like the Ingram-Dickson 'Aquaswift' 1411S Water Pump, for a contrived example. These turgid titles then find their way on to every piece of sales literature and every advertisement, hindering the layout man and bewildering the reader.

Firms who go in for this sort of thing labour under the delusion that their customers will somehow be impressed by the magnitude of it all – not least by the implication that Ingram-Dickson have made 141 previous water pump models, and this one is the latest development. Not so. First, even if true, it isn't believable; and in any case, this is a special product story and should be treated as such. Second, who gives a monkey's? Not me for one. As long as *this* model does what its makers claim, it's really academic how many they have made in the past.

For my money, they should make their minds up and call it either the Ingram-Dickson Water Pump, or the Aquaswift Water Pump, or the 1411S Water Pump. And leave it at that. Better still, they should call this one the Aquaswift and then give totally different names (Hydrosprite, and so on) to any other models which come along later.

The simpler a product name, the easier it is to remember and the less bothersome to ask for. That's the object of the exercise, isn't it?

Also on the identity/image front is the standard of your company stationery and literature, the look of the firm's vehicles and reception area, and the demeanour of your sales staff – with particular regard to your receptionist. All of these should be as attractive and personable as you can make them or hire them.

When a customer visits your premises and is forced to cool his heels for a few minutes in your reception area he is, in every respect, a captive audience. In that case, why not give him something to look at? Put up an interesting display of your products, your literature, even your advertising. And change it often.

Try, also, to develop a corporate identity. Adopt company colours and print and paint everything accordingly. Originate a house-style, complete with logotype where appropriate, and use it on all literature and stationery. Again, carry this corporate identity through to things like workers' overalls, caps, uniforms and badges. For what it costs, it's well worth the trouble. And even if your firm consists of only the proverbial man and dog, make sure the dog wears his company collar at all times.

If you see what I mean.

Your designer will know all about corporate image. Let him or her have *carte blanche* and you'll be spoilt for choice.

When launching a new product – though more specifically a new service – you may do well to consider holding a press-reception at a local hotel or, indeed, on your own premises. Either way, the idea behind it is to get as much media coverage as possible for the minimum amount of money spent.

These things take a bit of organizing; and you can never guarantee the strength of the attendance. But depending on how many invitations you send, the money spent is often worth the candle.

To do the job in any way properly, you will need a small army of stewards/salespeople to top up glasses and answer questions knowledgeably. Once more, you can hire people from a model agency for this job; but do brief them thoroughly before the event about your company and about what you expect them to do. The room you hire should be suitably decorated with display stands showing the product, or information boards outlining the company and the service. In addition, prepare a press-information pack – a press release, product brochures and/or photographs, a blurb giving a background of the company – and have a copy handed to each guest on admission.

At some strategic point during the evening (always hold press receptions in the *early* evening, or around lunchtime), a company spokesman should make a short statement about the purpose of the reception and the aims of the company. You might also consider running a short – a very short – audio-visual presentation.

Journalism is a notoriously thirsty profession, so provide ample quantities of wallop. And if your budget runs to it, arrange for a light buffet, too.

From then on, it's all in the lap of the gods. The coverage you get will depend on any number of hardly quantifiable circumstances. From experience, though, I can tell you that your journalist guests will do their best to play the game and, all things being equal, will publish favourable reports.

I don't imagine for a minute that it will be lost on you how these events provide an ideal opportunity to come face-to-face with existing and prospective customers.

I thought not.

7 Radio activity and TV screening

At the time of writing there are almost sixty commercial radio stations operating throughout the UK, and the nice aspect about this degree of choice is that each and every one of them is busting a gut to get its hands on your business – no matter how small you may be, nor how little the resulting revenue.

Because of this, radio advertising time has never been easier to buy; and, relatively speaking, has never been cheaper. As it happens, air-time salesmen are falling over themselves to do financial deals which, a few years ago, would have seemed laughable.

Why should this be so? Is it on account of radio advertising doesn't work? Doesn't perform as well as in some other countries? Or is it because the hassle involved in physically producing commercials is not worth the effort? The answer is no, on all three counts. Radio advertising does get results – big results. And the mechanics of putting a commercial together are now so straightforwad as to contain very little mystery.

The problem, from the radio station's point of view, lies in the stifling weight of the competition, plus the volume of material each needs to justify its existence. Radio is a great, hungry maw that devours material in copious quantities. Calculate a day's output on any station and the dreadful reality dawns. Once set in motion these organizations become as unstoppable as the apprentice's broomstick. The more they put out, the more they demand; and the clock ticks merrily away.

But all of this, luckily, is not our worry. Ours is to decide whether there is any value in putting our products or services on radio.

So here are the very basic facts of the matter.

During what is known as drive-time (approximately 7.00–9.00 a.m. and 3.00–6.00 p.m.), we can reach a fair mix of listeners. These will be predominently male, since they are travelling to and from work in cars, but their age-groupings of 18 to 65 makes them an ideal target for a wide range of sales pitches.

During the rest of the day, by and large, we shall be talking to the housebound – housewives, retired people, and such. There will, of course, be a proportion of the employed in this segment: people like mechanics, painters and decorators, hairdressers, and some factory workers – those who are able to work and listen at the same time.

The nature of our product, therefore, determines the times that any radio commercials we make are aired. There would be little point in promoting a new cosmetic – no matter how spectacularly inexpensive – at 6.30 a.m. when the audience is mainly men who have just left their beds and who are getting ready to face a day's work. Conversely, you wouldn't try to sell pints of beer at 11.00 a.m. to an audience which generally drinks nothing larger, or stronger, than a schooner of sherry.

However, things are not always this cut and dried; and it is imperative before marketing any product, no matter which gender the product appeals to, that you establish exactly *who makes the decision to buy*.

As any good car salesman will tell you, when he's selling to a married couple it's the man who makes the decision about the make and model of car, but it's invariably the woman who chooses the colour. She will have a very big say on the price, too. So in reality, she makes the *final* choice – the buying decision. (This, as you will appreciate, applies just as much to press advertising as it does to radio commercials.)

Once again, then, timing is all important. So is pin-pointing the market with respect to hitting the right audience at the right time. A little research will help you to work this out fairly precisely. And don't be talked into buying air-time slots outside your market segment on the

LAMANCHA RADIO

Monday to Friday

Basic rates

Time	Classification	20 seconds	30 seconds	40 seconds	50 seconds	60 seconds
6 a.m.–9 a.m.	B1	£106.00	£132.00	£172.00	£218.00	£238.00
9 a.m.–12 noon	B2	£79.00	£99.00	£129.00	£163.00	£178.00
12 noon–3 p.m.	B3	£32.00	£40.00	£52.00	£66.00	£72.00
3 p.m.–6 p.m.	B4	£24.00	£30.00	£39.00	£50.00	£54.00
6 p.m.–midnight	B5	£5.25	£6.50	£8.50	£10.50	£11.50

New advertiser bonus

Bonus air-time to the value of 25 per cent of the initial order is available to all advertisers who are new to Lamancha Radio, or who have not advertised with us within the previous two years. The bonus is available for up to twenty-six consecutive weeks from the date of the first transmission.

Fixed spots

Subject to availability, advertisers may 'fix' their spots, when booked at basic rates, within a particular programme or quarter-hour time segment by paying a 25 per cent surcharge on the appropriate rate.

● Rates shown are 'per spot' and exclusive of VAT.

● 10-second spots are available at 50 per cent of the 30-second rate.

● Spots will be evenly rotated across time segments and days of the week.

● Local rates are available to advertisers whose business is conducted wholly or mainly within the Lamancha Radio transmission area, and are at the discretion of Lamancha Radio.

Commercial production

The above advertising rates are exclusive of production costs. A full list of rates is available on request.

grounds that they are cheaper and that you will get more of them. This is a useless, false economy.

Your air-time salesman will give you all the facts and figures. Also, he will, if he's any good, help you to locate your audience. And when it comes to talking about the actual cost of your campaign, haggle a little. You may take my word for it that most radio-reps are allowed some degree of licence on costs. They can come and go on prices; and to be honest about it, they would rather have your business at a reduced rate than not have it at all.

Here's a mock-up station rate card (p. 125) to give you some idea of the numerous timings and costings. This card is very much simplified and does not include items such as: special package rates, weekend broadcasting rates, etc.

Do I need to tell you that you buy radio air-time in seconds? Oh, all right, then. It comes in segments of 20, 30, 40, 50 and 60 seconds. As you can see from the rate card, the cost-per-spot varies dramatically according to the time of day it is aired. You will also notice that the B5 rates are virtual give aways – until you realize that the station has *carte blanche* to slot you in wherever and whenever it feels like it, between the 6.00 p.m. to midnight period. So you could end up going out when almost everyone is glued to a television set watching *Dallas*, and when the rest are unconscious through sleep or drink. Which is why the shorter time-slots during drive-time (especially morning drive-time) are the more expensive.

Hopefully, the rest of it speaks for itself.

What about the mechanics of making radio commercials? Can they be produced by the ordinary businessman in the street? And can they be made without recourse to the services of a radio-production company?

Well, yes they can. But then, again, no they can't. The fact of the matter is you can do both.

However, before we get too deeply involved in the whys and wherefores, perhaps a touch of background is in order.

Given a half-decent script, any commercial radio station worthy of the name will make a competent spot for you. What's more, if you are prepared to spend enough on air-time many of them will not only make the commercial free of charge, they will also write the script – absolutely gratis.

But assuming that the money available is not sufficient to engender this kind of service, there are two ways to be certain that your production receives the input it deserves. Either write it yourself and insist upon being at the recording session in order to monitor what stays in and what gets thrown out. Or, if you categorically cannot face putting pen to paper, buy the labour of a professional copywriter. (You'll know how to go about hiring a writer from Chapter 5.) He or she will be delighted to put a workable script together; and just about all of them can handle a recording session without too much trouble. Though if you're in any doubt about the latter, check out their reputation with other people in the trade.

I know of one very able writer who is a notoriously bad radio producer. His philosophy is to stamp his personality upon studio engineers and voice-over artists from the outset and generally show them who the governor is. The net result is a lot of upset and all-round frustration – not to say a portfolio of mediocre commercials. The way I see it, there is but one way to conduct a studio session – the easy way. I'll describe it in a moment or two.

Before that, may I bend your ear in defence of the poor old copywriter? Can I say that copywriters have a truly rotten job? I'll explain.

When they are not producing advertising (and if they are wholly dependent upon freelancing, this is most of the time), they will be knocking out plays for Radio 4, or short stories for *Woman's Own*, or novels for anybody. None of which is ever likely to see itself published, by the way.

So put yourself in their shoes, ponder their tribulations, and consider whether you would wish to live the hiding-to-nothing life they are forced to exist. To start with they are in the manufacturing business, since putting squiggles on paper could be loosely described as manufacturing. Next, they are also in the mail-order business, because every manuscript is sent away to a publisher 'on approval'.

To pile Pelion upon Ossa, they then have to wait for as long as six months for a yes or no decision – which inevitably turns out no. (I am reliably informed that publishers use unwanted manuscripts for hamster-bedding.)

It is, I would argue, a situation up with which no manufacturer or mail-order merchant would put. They would neither tolerate it, nor could they survive it.

Not only that, the copywriter is hampered by a largely national practice of literacy. Just about everyone owns a pen, and very few are reluctant to use it when presented with a piece of advertising copy which has been written on their behalf. To cut the matter short, people aren't slow in coming forward to alter, edit, re-hash, even re-write the copywriter's efforts. To put it even crisper, they believe it to be their divine right.

Sadly, all too many of them are allowed to get away with it. But we bolder souls, those of us who are prepared to stand up and tell them where the bus stops, hold to the conviction that a decent copywriter very nearly sweats blood in the execution of his job. And nobody – let's be fair – should expect to transfuse a fellow human without him kicking up a modest dust.

Therefore, please be kind to the copywriter. Treat him or her right and they will treat you like a king. That's a promise.

Anyhow, it will be an advantage if you know what goes into one of these sessions and understand the production techniques and the functions of the people involved.

★   ★   ★

Radio production

There are two kinds of recording studio. The one operated by a radio station, and the other privately owned: the radio-production company. Each makes an hourly charge for studio use. At the time of writing, this is somewhere around £35 to £50 an hour.

Generally speaking, radio station studio time is cheaper

than that of the independent concerns. This doesn't make them better – just cheaper. Almost all of the latter are heavily involved in music-album production. Which is why, on any given day of the week, the average studio is running alive with hopeful young musicians. And this, from your angle, is a good thing – as you will discover shortly. The making of commercials, therefore, is often only a sideline.

It will come as no surprise to you, though, that compiling an album requires a high degree of technical skill. Thus, the engineers and the equipment they use are sometimes thought to be of a higher standard than is generally found in the average radio station, where little more is demanded than the broadcasting of pre-recorded music and voice-links. In my experience this is not necessarily the case.

A studio engineer, any studio engineer, should be considered a friend. His know-how and advice must be taken into account on all matters; and when he says he has heard a 'pop on the mike' (when the voice-over artist has over-pronounced the letter p), or if he suggests that the sibilance is altogether too sharp, do take his word for it – even if you still fail to notice the error after several replays.

In privately run studios, the engineer is often the owner of the establishment. This being the case, he wants to do the finest possible job for you. Let him see your script in advance of the recording session. Allow him to suggest a particular voice-over artist for the job – of which he will usually have a considerable stable. And if he advises the use of background music, take the recommendation seriously. At least, do him the honour of listening to a run-through of the pre-recorded library music he has chosen, side-by-side with the voice over.

Library music, incidentally, comes in a wide range of specialist labels and in an exhaustive choice. Jazz, rock, light orchestral, heavy orchestral and what are known as novelty numbers. Most studios keep a comprehensive stock of library music – as well as a collection of sound-effects discs.

Now, library music, unlike ordinary recorded music, is

written and produced specifically for commercial use. In this respect it is not bound by the normal copyright laws of recorded music, which state that unauthorized use is very likely to result in a costly court action. With library music, as with sound effects, you simply pay a small fee and it's yours to use. The studio keeps track of all library music employed and makes returns to the appropriate copyright body.

Fees? The current rate for music is around £40 per commercial, per station. Sound effects weigh in at about £10 a go. I'll clarify that. If you make one commercial to be aired on one specific station over a period, £40 is the total payment for music (or £10 per sound effect) for the duration of that period. However, if you are running on more than one station, the fee increases to £40 multiplied by the number of stations. Furthermore, should you re-run the commercial at some later date, you'll be expected to stump up another fee.

But this is cheap compared with what you might pay for 'proprietory' recordings – always supposing you can get permission to utilize them. Many composers won't allow their music to be used for commercial purposes under any circumstances. I once asked Alan Price for use of that superb piece *Just for You* for a butchery chain.. He turned me down flat. I can't say that I blame him.

An alternative to library music is custom-written music. There are two ways to put this together.

1   Employ a specialist jingle-production company and expect to pay anything from £2,000 for the composition and recording – plus a fee for the number of airings it will receive.
2   Write it yourself.

I assure you that writing it yourself is not as difficult as it may seem on face value. To do this, you don't have to be a musician as such, because once you have an idea for a tune, you can get all the help you need to arrange the piece. And it's the arranging of a tune that makes the writing seem such a hallowed precinct.

There is, unhappily for them, but fortunately for you, a

vast army of musicians in every town who are not employed as fully as they might wish. That applies, again sadly, to even the best of them. Most of these people will be in touch with your local recording studio on a day-to-day basis, and can be readily located.

A professional keyboard player will arrange a tune from a basic idea consisting of less than a dozen notes of music for as little as £60. For this, he puts the entire music side of the jingle together: the melody line; harmony; and the basic chords for whatever instruments you intend to use. His recording session fee, for which he rehearses, leads and pays a group of three or so musicians and/or a vocalist, should not come to more than £400 all up.

Barring accidents, production time for a jingle shouldn't exceed two to three hours. Say, £150 studio time. Add an hour's mixing time – when the engineer monitors and corrects the sound-levels of the various instruments, and commits them all to a master-tape – and you've got yourself a jingle for less than £700.

Clearly, producing your own words and music for jingles is not only cheaper, but considerably more satisfying. Better still, you also have total control of the end product – it's yours and yours alone. Logically, in your dealings with musicians, you will negotiate a 'buy-out' fee. This fee is the overall cost of their services and represents full and final payment – there are no repeat fees or 'per station' fees to worry about.

Buying out, too, is by far the best way to commission voice-over artists; and for the very same reason. But it always pays to be fair and reasonable with these people, no matter how hungry you feel they may be. As members of Equity, which they must be to go broadcastable, they are fairly well protected. Even so, some will readily agree to do the work at less than union rate, either out of necessity or as a favour to you. Whatever the situation, I advise you to remember that they know their jobs better than you do. Treat them right and you'll get more than your money's worth – a lot more.

When employing a professional voice-over artist, do bear

the following in mind. First, make sure you get a voice to fit the script. In other words, if it's a humorous piece, commission an actor who is used to humour, or who is at least able to interpret and deliver a funny line without sounding awkward. You can find the correct voice – male or female – by listening to the studio's pre-recorded bank of artists. They will almost certainly have demonstration tapes for the purpose.

Having chosen the voice, let him or her see the script before you go into the studio. This way, you avoid time-wasting and money-wasting delays for script changes where the artist is unable, for one reason or another, to properly deliver certain passages. Difficulty is usually experienced when the writer is unfamiliar with the artist's style of delivery, or when the script is burdened by cumbersome alliteration. Furthermore, should your voice-over suggest making certain script changes – and if they don't physically affect the strength of the message – then make those changes. He will have a better idea than most about what sounds acceptable to the ear.

Always keep it in the back of your mind, too, that a professional actor has a standard to maintain. He won't wish to appear in a bad commercial any more than you'll want to produce one. He has trained in microphone techniques; he knows about inflection and breath control; and he has made a study of pace and timing. It's called skill and it is not given half the respect it deserves.

The going rate for a standard voice-over is about £70 an hour, or per script. You make your own arrangements; but the per hour rate is far better, since a good VO can put down two or three scripts in an hour. For a personality, you can be talking astronomical sums: £25,000 for a day's work isn't unheard of. It all depends, of course, on how popular the artist is at the time.

Commissioning a big name to endorse your product can pay big dividends – even if the name you use is only a local one, like a DJ, or a presenter from a regional radio station, or a star from the town's football club. Though person-alities can bring problems. Use a big name who is just about to get himself nicked for using drugs, or who walks out on his wife and five kids in favour of a leggy blonde, and you might just as well cut your losses, scrap the commercial, and start all over. Or cut your throat.

On this subject, you may feel the urge to employ a personality from a well-known radio or TV show. With his or her acquiescence, you write a script that's complete with catchphrases and names of characters from the show. Fantastic, you reckon. But I say: don't do it. The writers of said show, if they ever hear your piece on the air, will rightly get the hump. Even if they don't sue you – which I would judge to be not so much an outside chance as an evens favourite – there's good reason to believe that they will invoice you in a big way.

By using elements from their show, you have infringed their copyright. And there's only one bigger sin than pinching a writer's bread and butter, and that's stealing his beer.

We shall now say something about the equipment you are likely to find at the recording studio.

Most private studios will provide anything from 8-track to 32-track recording; while radio stations proper are normally only 2-track or, at best, 4-track. The principle is that the more tracks available to you, the more individual pieces of sound can be overlaid, side by side, one after the other. To be fair to radio stations, they don't need such sophisticated equipment in their operations. But the fact remains, the more the better. So you can lay down an initial voice-bed, say, and then add music or sound effects at will. Or vice versa. Indeed, in this way, just a single musician using a synthesizer or electronic keyboard, from which an illimitable range of sounds may be coaxed, can put down numerous separate tracks to build a complete orchestral feel – with melody line, harmonies and fillers.

This procedure, it may be judged, will save the cost of a full complement of musicians. It will, however, take longer to complete, and so your studio time-charges will increase in proportion.

* * *

At any rate, what you end up with at the end of a recording session is, physically speaking: two × ¼ in reel-to-reel magnetic tapes for each station you are appearing on. Stations demand two as an insurance against one becoming lost between sales-office and transmission-desk. (What happens in the event they lose both, I have no idea.) Your studio will despatch these to the station on your behalf, or you can deliver them yourself.

Ask the engineer and your commercial will be stored on a 2 in master-tape at the studio – just to guard against loss. You may be asked to pay a small fee for this service. Should you envisage making a number of commercials over a period, suggest that the studio sells you a personal master-tape. Cost? About £30; and then you'll have enough recording room to store commercials for the next twenty years. Ordinary cassette copies, for playing in the privacy of your own home, can be run off for about a fiver each.

What about the actual length – the timing – of commercials? It stands to reason, doesn't it, that having booked a series of 30-second spots, the commercials you produce to fill them should be 30 seconds long. Any scripts you write, therefore, should be timed with some accuracy. On no account use the second hand of a watch for this purpose – use a proper stop-watch.

I assure you that not too many people are able to make their timings spot-on before the event; because one man's read-through of a script is unlikely to match another man's. Even so, you can write it as near as dammit exact; and any over-matter (of which there will no doubt be plenty in your early attempts) can be edited out during the recording. Alternatively, the studio may possess a clever electronic device via which a voice may be imperceptibly speeded up so as to fit the allocated time.

A word in your ear. Should the piece run *under* time, and you and everybody else is happy with the sound of it, then the best course is to leave it short. The jazzing around involved in trying to make up a couple of seconds is seldom worth the effort. When you think about it, you are losing nothing. If the commercial is good, that extra fraction of time won't make it any better.

★   ★   ★

I said I'd tell you how to conduct a studio session – so I suppose I better had.

As it happens, I have a reputation for being very laid back, even couldn't care less, at these events. It's partly earned. I must confess. I don't know about you, but when I employ professionals, I expect the job to be done accordingly – with style and with not a little panache. So I leave the problems of levels, mixing and timings to the engineering staff. I also allow the voice-over artist to get on with his trade in the best way he knows how. Methinks this attitude gives me an altogether better job in the end.

The practice of going for take after take in the hope of 'getting something better' is, in my far from trivial judgement, a slight on everybody concerned. And in a tense situation, things tend to get measurably worse rather than become moderately improved.

If a voice-over is unable to get the piece into the can within, say, three or four takes, either you've chosen the wrong VO, or your initial briefing to him was a bad one. I cannot, offhand, think of any other reason.

And here lies the secret behind all radio production – the standard of the initial briefing. Always run through the script with engineer and VO. Tell them exactly what it is you are looking for in terms of pace, delivery and intonation. Make it clear, right from the outset whether you want a lot of bass or timbre in the voice. Set them straight on the pronunciation of proper names or of any uncommon words. Explain to the artist the nuances of any sound effects you have elected to use; and let him hear any backing music.

Then allow them to get on with it. And try to interfere as little as your ego will permit.

Providing you have chosen the right people – and if you haven't, it's nobody's fault but your own – you might just as well toddle off to the pub for an hour. It is not, I think, unreasonable to allow people who can do a job a darn sight better than you can, to do it without interruption.

In my minor experiment with radio, I have worked with unknown (to coin a phrase) voices and top entertainers alike. From jobbing actors to the highly-skilled likes of Vincent Price, Terry Wogan, Leonard Rossiter and Valentine Dyall, among others. Who the hell would I be to tell any of *them* how to deliver a line?

The question is rhetorical.

The dos and don'ts of radio work would, without question, fill a book of their own. (If anyone asks, and if the money is right, maybe I'll write it.) However, a good many of them are also apposite to television work. For that reason, I'll leave radio right here and move on to TV where, with any luck, I shall be able to complete the picture.

★   ★   ★

Television advertising

You may feel, and perhaps rightly, that a section on television commercials is somewhat ambitious in a book which purports to talk to low-budget advertisers about low-budget advertising. In defence of its inclusion, however, there are a couple of observations I should make.

From experience, low-budget advertisers often end up as medium or large-budget advertisers; especially when they get their initial campaigns right. Allow me to give you an applicable example.

A certain restaurant-franchise operator started off no more than five years ago with one outlet and an advertising budget which you could have placed in your eye and winked. Not the sort of bloke to bother about such trifles, he made a simple, 20-second TV commercial, which cost him in the region of £1,200, and bought air-time to the tune of £5,000. This may seem a lot of money, but in air-time terms, it's a mere bagatelle. At any rate, the campaign worked; and it worked to such effect that it not only brought hungry customers to his tables, it also motivated franchisees to open their own restaurants under his banner.

The footnote is that this man currently operates nearly two dozen franchise outlets and spends a tidy £160,000 a year on advertising them. Not only that, he has the turnover to justify it.

Come the day that you are tempted, probably by some over-enthusiastic station rep, to buy television time, you'll be better off for having a working knowledge of the medium. A lot better off.

Too many advertisers leap into the television saddle not knowing a tracking shot from a clapperboard and, consequently, get their fingers bitterly burned.

In the advertising scheme of things, television is most certainly the hardest selling of all the media. There can be no real doubt about it. Television also has the added benefit of visual stimulation; the attraction of immediacy; and the advantage of reaching your audience – your very much captive audience – in the relaxed atmosphere of their own homes.

But even prisoners still retain a mind of their own; and the average viewer can spot a rotten commercial three streets away. So there's more to making TV spots than simply matching a few words with a series of pictures, airing the result as often as money allows, and hoping that you will shortly be able to call the Rio Sheraton with a block-booking.

Provably, a bad television commercial, unlike bad radio or press, can be so completely destructive to your cause, so thoroughly off-putting to your audience, that it will refuse to touch your product under any circumstances.

Therefore, before venturing on to the box, seek advice from the production staff of the TV station in question, or from the principals of an independent film-production house. Each of these will be eager to show you what they have done for others, and to tell you exactly what was involved in terms of time and money.

Here are a few pointers to take on board:

1   As a new business advertiser, you should be able to negotiate preferential rates for radio and television time.
2   Establish all studio production costs at the outset and remember that time represents money.
3   Research your market to ensure that the timings of commercials correspond with the listenership or viewership of the audience you wish to reach. (The stations will have this information.)
4   Whether you use a freelance writer, or write the script yourself, research the piece among people whom you can trust to give you an honest opinion.
5   Before using suggested library music, find out if anyone (especially a competitor) is currently using it. In which case, choose an alternative.
6   Remember that having an actor 'on screen' will cost more than using him as a non-appearing voice-over.
7   Be selective in your choice of voice-over artist. It is a mistake to use somebody who is 'over-exposed', or who is employed by a competitor.
8   Where possible, negotiate a 'buy-out' fee with voice-overs and musicians.
9   Never try to say too much in a commercial. Simplicity is the keyword.

★   ★   ★

Let's now talk about the nuts and bolts of making a TV spot. There are, in essence, five ways of producing a commercial.

1   35 mm live-action film.
2   35 mm rostrum-camera using still photographs and/or optical devices and captions.
3   35 mm animation.
4   VTR (video tape recording) as live-action.
5   VTR made solely on an electronic control panel, incorporating stills and/or special visual techniques.

Allow me to briefly explain all of that.
1   Live-action is exactly what the term implies. You go

to a location, or build a set, and shoot 'live'. This can be done with either lip-synchronization sound, which records the voices of your artists on-the-spot; or as a mute shoot with voices and effects dubbed on after the event.

2 Rostrum camera is a 35 mm camera mounted over a horizontal table upon which stills and/or artwork are placed and shot. This method is obviously a good deal cheaper than live-action. The illusion of movement may be achieved by scanning the photographs, or by tracking in and out of focal features, and by dissolving one still into the next.

3 Animation, again, speaks for itself; but this kind of work can be inordinately expensive. The two or three animation houses of any worth in the UK employ top-line animators and cartoonists who cannot be bought for buttons. So it stands to reason that they will charge heavily for their services. A good animation commercial, though, can be worth its weight in gold. It won't date the way live-action dates (clothes and hairstyles change rapidly, remember), and so it can be run year after entertaining year.

Way back I wrote and produced an animation spot for a well-known biscuit manufacturer. It incorporated a jingle based, incidentally, on the *Sorceror's Apprentice* theme. By some pleasant happenstance, it became so popular with youngsters that we were urged to make a give-away, flimsy-disk recording of the tune. If nothing else, this example shows the pulling power of animated work.

4, 5 VTR next; and even as you read what I have to say, what I have to say will be out of date – all compliments of the microchip. Suffice it to tell you that with VTR, you can do anything that can be done with film; and then some. For rapidly produced optical work it cannot be beaten. Whereas film has to be processed in a laboratory, and while opticals such as split-screen, superimpositions, dissolves, wipes, revolves, spins and tumbles need much time and technical work to achieve, VTR will accomplish any or all of these techniques in a matter of seconds.

It follows that a VTR commercial can be far less expensive than the film version. However, while many TV stations are equipped with all the VTR bells and whistles and will happily make your spot at a moderate cost, just as many aren't. Given that your station is among the unfortunate latter, you will be forced to take your business to a private enterprise. And here's the rub. Just because it can manufacture a product cheaply, private enterprise (being the profit-motivated system it is) will not necessarily retail that product cheaply. Not if it has any sense it won't, anyway. This happens to be very much the situation with VTR production companies. They believe they have a sound, viable, buyable commody and they hold the view that it should be sold on the basis of its value to you, not the cost to them. One way around paying over the odds is to approach a fully-equipped TV station outside your area (assuming your regional TV station isn't fully-equipped), have the commercial made there, and ask them to 'pipe it down the line', i.e. transfer it to your regional station over the VTR network. Some will do this – some won't; it all depends on how badly they need the revenue for making it. But if you don't ask, you don't get a cheap commercial.

If pressed, I would say that generally speaking VTR is the choice for cheapness; although there are many situations where its use simply isn't practicable – like on many outdoor locations, or where a substantial amount of editing of takes is necessary. VTR can be edited, of course, but the process is expensive. What's more, I hold that 35 mm film gives a far superior production quality. I'm driven, none the less, to suspect that before any of us gets much older, VTR will supersede film in every aspect.

The foregoing is basically all you need to know about the methods of making commercials. There are, you will gather, no creative limits to which these methods may be put; and the visual variations on any of the given themes are limitless. You will doubtless be prepared to investigate a fair proportion of them at the proper moment.

Anyway, before you go haring off to a production company or TV studio, have a script put together. Better still, draft it yourself. Nobody can name a production price unless they have something to work from: an approximate idea of the sort of film you are aiming to make. This doesn't have to be a finished script, or a shooting script with the various scenes accurately timed out. All you need is a very rough draft. Any decent production house or station will tidy it up for you as part of the service. What they won't be able to do, in that event, is bounce you with a 'concept' fee, since the bones of it will be of your origination.

From that point on, once you've agreed costs, leave it to the professionals. By all means put them right on matters which relate specifically to your business, but by no means voice doubts about *their* side of the business. And never suggest making script changes mid-shoot.

Commercial film directors are exceptionally talented types. I've never yet met one who wasn't prepared to jump through hoops to give value for money. Almost certainly, too, the director on your minor epic will not feel he has done a proper job unless he can recommend more interesting ways of interpreting your script.

My advice is that you should listen to him. Carefully.

*   *   *

I'm sure you'll go along with me when I say that some television commercials are so dreadful, so utterly embarrassing, that you begin to wonder whether you, in fact, are the stupid one and must be missing some all-too-subtle and salient point. You aren't, of course, but you can't help thinking it.

The material I refer to is invariably advertising a brand of soap powder, or a domestic cleanser. Not all of them mind, just a terrible and frequent few. Are you with me?

The cost of producing and airing these commercials staggers the mind. Accumulatively, it would be sufficient to finance the first British moon-shot, and still have change left over for a civilized night out at Annabelle's. So we are forced to wonder why all this cash is chucked away for no other reason than to alienate people?

It appears that the companies who go in for such egregious rubbish believe, rightly, that constant repetition of a message – no matter how banal that message may be – will eventually bash the sentiments of it into the viewer's subconscious. They then go on to assume, quite wrongly as it turns out, that such brainwashing will motivate people to buy the product. It would be difficult, however, to make their error clear and to disillusion them on this score.

Am I trying to tell you that I know better than the marketeers of the multi-million pound conglomerates? Well, yes, as a matter of fact, I am. But you may take it or leave it as you wish.

What I am warning you against, in any commercial you make, is this vogue for the constant repetition of a company name or of a product name. Or, indeed, of a 'catch-line' relating to either.

You know the sort of thing I mean: *When the label says frigid, and the dirt stays rigid . . . New Brave gets 'em clean,* repeated *ad nauseum* throughout the commercial.

The point is, it's not always the big boys who go in for puerilities of this nature. Quite small advertisers, producers of infrequent 10- and 20-second spots do it, too. They reckon – without verifying a single fact – that the soap companies must know what they are doing, so they begin to emulate them. In the process, they help send the daft bandwaggon even faster downhill than it's already going. Then they wonder why their commercials fall upon deaf ears, and why the promotion falls flat on its face.

Don't do it, I say. We won't, you reply. On account of we can't afford it.

But you can afford it – that's the whole argument; and being able to afford it, you may be similarly tempted. You see, a swift video commercial employing a limbo background (i.e. with no set as such; it's shot in an open studio with no evident horizon) can be made amazingly cheaply. For some people it is too cheap for their own good. Most TV stations, as we've discussed, will sell you studio time – often for as little as £300 a hour. And when you discover that a straight 'presenter'-type commercial can be made in about two hours, it's clear that things are not as expensive as might have been imagined.

So we had better take another look at this, hadn't we?

As a small business advertiser, you don't have the insurance that the multi-nationals have. You cannot brandish millions of pounds as a justification for idiotic commercials. You cannot duck behind a paid for respectability. Neither can you hope that people will believe you know what you are doing, just because you are doing it like the soap giants. As a great old friend of mine so succinctly put it: 'Only the rich can afford poor advertising'. From the word go, your cheaply made and infrequent commercial will be seen for what it is. The work of a small company. In which case, your stuff had better be above reproach and neither offend, talk down to, nor annoy a single potential customer. It will have to work harder, speak more emotively, win more friends. You haven't a hope of matching the saturation coverage of the conglomerates, so your widely-spaced commercial must do a keener selling job. Try it the other way and it will be wasted.

I can site any number of instances where small firms have attempted it – and failed miserably. To find examples of your own, watch the 10-second slides and the 20-second spots which appear at the tail-end of break segments; and particularly those found on the farther-flung, regional stations. The bulk of these are, in a word, frightful; and this frightfulness is made considerably worse by the fact of them often being read 'live' by the station's duty announcer. Not *everything* is pre-recorded.

Now I have nothing whatsoever against station announcers, but whatever else they may be, commercial voice-over artists they most decidedly ain't. By virtue of their job, which is to disseminate programme information lucidly and precisely, their normal delivery is slow, detached and, quite often, wooden. However, when given a live commercial to deliver, their professional instincts indicate to them that they should somehow distinguish between it and the normal station announcements. Consequently, they raise their voices. More correctly, they holler down the mike in the mistaken belief that doing so will create the illusion of excitement.

It never does.

I reproduce a chimerical 10-second slide to illustrate what I've been saying, and also to show you what *not* to do. This effort might be pre-recorded, or station read. Either way, it's a nerve-tautening example of the genre which should be avoided at all costs.

Opening still picture of a bedroom scene

VO   'Johnson's Bedding Centre,' it screams. 'For duvets, quilt-covers and bed-linen.'
'Johnson's Bedding Centre,' it repeats. 'For quality bedroom furniture.'

End-board still picture of bedroom – complete with address line

'Johnson's Bedding Centre,' it yells once more. 'Anchor Street, Carlisle. See you there!'

Apart from being so irritating that one would be moved to chuck the telly out of the window, it has a further major fault. It suffers from too many words.

In a 10-second spot, only 8½ seconds are available for dialogue or soundtrack; for technical reasons, the initial 1½ seconds are mute; and this applies to all commercials regardless of length. The full 10 seconds is always available for the video – the picture. This being the case, then twenty words should be the absolute maximum for a 10-second spot. Clearly, these need to be twenty well-chosen words – certainly better chosen than those above and those I am griping about.

A surfeit of words renders the piece unintelligible; which is, when you think about it, insulting to the viewer. And to insult someone in their own home is the height of bad manners.

As you move into commercials of longer duration, you can afford to write more words per second. This is because a good voice-over artist, once in his stride, can handle three words a second comfortably and without sounding rushed. I imagine it has something to do with the second law of thermodynamics, or verbal inertia, or something. The fact remains: the longer the spot, the more you can say per second.

There is, of course, a saturation point beyond which it is impossible to venture; but you'll recognize it when you reach it. Not that you should even try to reach it. Some of the finest commercials ever produced have contained not a single word of dialogue. Television is, when all is said and done, a visual medium. You should do everything possible to keep it like that.

In addition to all of this, far too many short spots go out their way to be clever and tricky beyond their capabilities. They use impractical optical devices which take up valuable paid-for time unnecessarily. Any TV producer will tell you that for a 10-second commercial, one well-shot still photograph plus 'end-board' caption (address details, telephone, etc.) is five times more acceptable to the eye than five hastily-flashed opticals. The following general rule holds true for all spots, regardless of length: *Always give the eye time to adjust to a fresh visual situation.* Three seconds is about the minimum. And when cutting from scene to scene (i.e. from new situation to new situation), no scene deserves to be less than five seconds duration. Thus, novelty opticals of spins, revolves, tumbles, and so on, should last for three or more seconds; and pure scenes should be given at least five seconds to establish themselves.

Try not to confuse the viewer with a busy-busy video output. That doesn't mean you shouldn't strive to be creative. On the contrary, these short spots beg for creative ideas – since time, money and just about everything else is working against them.

Whatever you do in television, keep it simple.

★ ★ ★

Any script – television or radio – that you are planning to run, will need 'copy clearance' from the ITCA/AIRC Copy Secretariat. This is a body funded by independent broadcasters and monitors all commercials on independent stations. What they look for, and refuse clearance to, are overt sexual references, vulgarity, racist propaganda, violence, political bias, and downright untruths about a product or service. They also dislike associations of virility or manhood with beer-drinking, and any signs of over-indulgence.

Their address is Knighton House, 56 Mortimer Street, London, W1N 8AN. Telephone: 01 636 6866. You can either contact them off your own bat – and I assure you, they are the most helpful people – or you can leave it to the station which is to broadcast your piece. Whatever the case, make sure it's done at script stage. Don't wait for the commercial to be made before approaching them, or else you could be in for a very expensive disappointment. Be warned, the ITCA/AIRC can put a stop on your work that has a finality equal to a message of *bon voyage* from the Mafia.

Herewith, a list of film-production terms, along with their definitions. They may be of some use to you on the big day.

Cut   Instant change of scene.

Dissolve   The image (or scene) is dissolved out and the following scene dissolved in.

ECU   Extreme close-up.

Freeze frame   The freezing of an image and producing, to all intents and purposes, a still photograph.

Match dissolve   The image is dissolved from the subject in one location to the same subject in another location.

MCU   Medium close-up.

Mix   Where two scenes are briefly superimposed – the second slowly taking prominence.

Mvo   Male voice over.

Pan   The camera scans the subject from left to right, or vice versa.

SFX   Sound effects.

Super   Superimposing words (or another picture) over the original image.

Tracking shot   Where the camera moves along a track parallel to, towards, or away from the subject.

VO Voice over.

Wipe Changing from one scene to another without cutting. The image is 'blacked out' by panning the camera on to a black object.

Zoom Changing quickly from distance to close-up in one continuous movement.

8 Write your own material

This is not going to be easy. I cannot teach you how to write. More properly, I cannot teach you how to think. Because, when it's analysed, writing copy – for ads, sales letters, flyers, commercials, or whatever – is more about thinking than it is about writing.

It's about thinking how your product or service is better than any other product or service. About questioning exactly why this is so. And about dreaming up attractive ways of delivering these sellable differences. Back in Chapter 3, I attempted to convey how copy should, in its fight for attention, present itself. I now propose to offer methods of getting it down on paper.

To do that, we shall be obliged to adopt some hypothetical products. We'll analyse them, and their markets, then cobble together some press ads, a mail-shot and a radio commercial. This should show us how the various solutions are arrived at.

First, a necessary diversion. I've said it before, and I'll jolly-well say it again: when writing copy, strive for clarity. Use short words in simple phrases; and lay them out in a logical, easy-to-follow order. Grammar doesn't come into it. You won't need to be a grammarian to write copy, just a communicator. Feel free to begin your sentences with 'and' and 'but'; don't worry too much about splitting infinitives or mixing metaphors. Sentences don't have to be true sentences. Phrases like: 'Who says?' or 'Care to know more?' will sit perfectly comfortably on their own, and will give you a premeditated opportunity to qualify them with a relevant point such as: 'Our customers say. And you can read their unsolicited comments any time.' or 'All you have to do is ask. We'll send the facts and figures by return.'

Do you follow my drift that tightly-phrased questions like these open the door to all kinds of sales points? And that they save a whole lot of turgid explanatory detail?

I knew you would.

Copy is a language all its own; a kind of colloquial shorthand. As such, it should never be judged by the normal rules of English grammar – though, very stupidly, it quite often is.

Enough of that, let's get on and write something.

We know – don't we – that before writing a single word, we must first establish the unique selling proposition of the product. The one thing, or combination of things, that make it a better buy, a more useful buy, or a cheaper buy than anything being produced by our competitors. All right – so now we sit down to devise a creative strategy. An umbrella concept that can be used throughout the advertising campaign.

In effect, we write some headline concepts which include, explore and demonstrate the perceived USP.

To illustrate the thought process involved, I shall ask you to imagine that you are the proprietor of an estate agency which, as part of its service, offers a property management operation. It so happens, then, that you have a large shop premises on your books which is proving difficult to lease. The property is situated in one of the more salubrious areas of London – Baker Street, no less; and number 221b, to be tiresomely precise.

Try as you might, you cannot find a prospective leasee via the usual old-boy network; and this despite the fact that your client is offering a fat reduction on the first year's rental. This amounts to a substantial £50,000 off the asked for rent of £250,000. The market for such a property is the larger chain-stores and supermarkets.

Your only way out, it seems, is to go public; to run a few ads in the relevant retail-property publications.

The USP of the premises is, surely, the prestigious address; while the subsidiary selling point is the £50,000 rent reduction. Knowing this, we shall try to include both propositions in the headline:

IF YOU NEED SOME GOOD REASONS
FOR TAKING A LEASE
ON 221b BAKER STREET,
HERE ARE £50,000-WORTH

It seems to tell the story well enough; but does it have the punch to set the office phone ringing with anything like the urgency we require? Maybe a more obtuse tack will do the job.

I would say that the £50,000 reduction might fairly be described as a 'back-hander'. Therefore:

THE LEASE ON 221b BAKER STREET
HAS MORE BACKHAND
THAN WIMBLEDON FORTNIGHT

Doubtful. Even accompanied by a picture of an executive briefcase overflowing with banknotes, this may still not be strong enough. Patently, the previous disinterest in this property suggests saying and doing something fairly dramatic. A far better way of going about it, therefore, might be to illustrate, as large as possible, an ordinary, everyday bath-plug suspended from a chain. Superimposed around the rim of the plug would be the figure: £50,000. The headline could then run:

THERE'S A BIG BUNG WAITING
FOR THE NEW LEASEHOLDER
OF 221b BAKER STREET

To rich for your blood? You could be right; but at least you now have an understanding of what should be going on in your mind when formulating concepts. So let's devise some more marketing scenarios and produce headline concepts to answer them.

You are a shopkeeper and your establishment is contained within a new and largish shopping precinct that also houses some forty other traders. These range from a travel agent to a pet shop; from a computer centre to a cafeteria.

On account of you are a pretty intelligent soul, you have been democratically elected by the rest of the shopkeepers to prepare and handle the advertising for the group. Which means you are charged with promoting (a) the precinct, and (b) each of the shops within it.

We shall call it the Downtown Centre.

Now it stands to reason that if all forty shop proprietors are chipping in with money to finance the promotional work, each will wish to get a fair and equitable crack of the whip. Any outfit seen to be getting more attention than the rest (especially if it happens to be your outfit) will soon be pounced upon, denounced and swiftly brought to heel. Considering how many shops there are, giving equal weight and prominence to each isn't going to be easy.

The size of the budget allows you to run one 250 mm (10 in) by four columns ad in the local daily paper every other day for a month. This is not a launch ad, since the precinct has been open for some weeks. What it amounts to is a reminder ad to potential shoppers along the lines of: 'We're all here, open for business – come and get it.'

What do you make of it? The USP seems to be, basically, that all of said shops are conveniently housed under one roof. Apart from that, there is very little to say. You aren't offering collective price reductions; nor are you giving anything away as a 'come on'. Somehow, the campaign has to come from within the principle that a group of shops is better than a road of haphazardly scattered shops.

Fair enough. You should now let your mind wander over and around the USP in an effort to pinpoint an effective concept. You might kick off with a thought in this direction:

YOUR LOCAL DOWNTOWN STORE
IS 40 SHOPS BIG

With a line such as this, we should probably go on to list all forty shops and give some indication of their individual services. It will work at a pinch; though we could go a step farther with:

LIKE ALL GOOD STORES,
WE STOCK ALMOST EVERYTHING.
UNLIKE MOST, WE NEED
40 SHOPS TO STOCK IT IN

Again, we would list all the participating shops. It's getting closer, I feel – if a touch contrived. Would it not be a coup if we could put that list of shops into the headline? The whole lot in one huge statement?

WHERE ELSE CAN YOU GET
YOUR HAIR STYLED; YOUR HOLIDAY
BOOKED; A T-SHIRT PRINTED;
SWEETS WRAPPED; TRY ON CLOTHES;
CURTAIN WINDOWS; BUY FISH; MEAT;
BREAD AND GROCERIES; SEND FLOWERS;
RENT A TELEVISION;
CHOOSE A PET;
GET ENGAGED; HAVE YOUR PICTURE TAKEN;
KEY A COMPUTER; LINGER OVER LINGERIE;
FIT SHOES;
CUT A KEY; ADMIRE ANTIQUES;
BROWSE BOOKS; SELECT CHINA;
FURNISH YOUR HOME; AND THEN SIT DOWN
FOR A QUIET COFFEE . . .
ALL UNDER ONE ROOF?

THE DOWNTOWN CENTRE

Tidied up a touch – and double-checked that everybody is accounted for in one way or another – this line has all the makings of a good ad.

We'll move on.

You are now the manufacturer of a type of fishing line. This stuff comes in a range of thicknesses and strengths – from 1 kg to 50 kg breaking strain. For better or worse, this answer to every angler's dream is called Argonaut. Now Argonaut is made from a blend of polyamides which give it certain interesting qualities: (a) it does not bunch or tangle the way some lines are inclined to do; (b) unlike regular catgut, even unorthodox granny-type knots have a better chance of staying tied; (c) it has very little springiness when wound on to a reel – which means it isn't inclined to unwind itself from the spool. However, it does have considerable tensile 'give', thus it can better withstand vicious takes from large fish; (d) Argonaut will handle any kind of fish: game, coarse, or deep-sea.

Our ads for Argonaut are due to appear in the angling publications; and we are selling direct to the consumer.

Are you ready? Not really, you say. I know nothing about fishing. To be truthful, neither do I – never having got past the bent-pin worm-drowning stage. So what? I've never before allowed ignorance of a subject to stop me from going on about it at great length. Why should I start now?

The USP here appears to be the non-tangle, taking-the-strain element. It's a tough line that doesn't tangle. From what I can remember of my few days' fishing experience, I believe I spent the best part of the time unravelling great balls of matted line. Anyway, the market for Argonaut is the rugged, outdoor type who, like the average golfer, will do almost anything to improve his skill at the sport.

On those fundamentals, let's begin with a proposition like this:

ARGONAUT. THE ACTION LINE

Mmmm. What does it say, apart from nothing? Nothing. Then why not go bald-headed for the non-tangle aspect:

ARGONAUT. OTHERWISE YOU COULD SPEND THE DAY BIRD-NESTING

That's a little more like it. With an accompanying illustration of a frustrated angler endeavouring to sort out a monumental tangle, it would definitely get the attention we are looking for. But how many experienced fishermen find themselves in such a predicament? Not many, I fear. We would be better off exploring the tensility of the line and the 'give' side of the story.

How does this grab you?

ARGONAUT. THE STRONGEST LINE SINCE THE MASON-DIXON

Will it be understood? Possibly not. Is it asking too much of the reader? Almost certainly. Then a straight message with just a simple twist is the answer.

ARGONAUT. THE MORE IT GIVES, THE MORE YOU TAKE

Better by far. Placed in conjunction with a picture of an angler landing a large fish – the rod bent almost double – it promises to be an acceptable ad.

Do please forgive me if some of this appears a touch trite or a bit elementary. All I'm trying to do is demonstrate that there is more to writing an ad than leaping on to the first idea that happens to strike you. It must be obvious to anyone who isn't a raving looney that there are at least a dozen ways of presenting a basic sales pitch. And you, not being a raving looney, are bound to agree with me.

So I'm not saying for a moment that the above concepts are the only answers to the problems set. They are just a few of many – a very few. Indeed, I should be vastly disappointed if you haven't already come up with something far superior.

Be that as it very well may, those of you who have never before given a single thought to the making of ads will, I feel sure, be somewhat the wiser. But not wise enough, I hope, to have decided to leave this kind of work to the professionals. Before you make up your mind on this issue, I urge you to spend a moment or two in discovering how body copy proper is put together.

I'll start with a relatively simple example. It concerns the advertising of a carpet retailer – let's call it the Walkover Carpet Company. The brief runs thus:

1   The company retails a selection of more than 2000 types
    and patterns of carpet from a large discount warehouse.
    All of the merchandise is on display to the public. And
    prices start at £2 a square yard. (Herein lies the USP.)
2   It operates a free-of-charge, 24-hour delivery service.
    Alternatively, the customer can take the purchase away
    in his own transport.
3   The carpets are produced by twenty or so well-known
    manufacturers. However, Walkover Carpets' bulk-
    buying policy enables the company to sell at prices
    considerably lower than those of traditional carpet
    stores.
4   The company, not unexpectedly, gives free estimates,
    and also provides a free planning service. For a modest
    fee, it operates a fitting service which guarantees that
    carpets will be laid by an expert team within 24 hours of
    purchase.
5   Walkover Carpets is open 7 days a week, 9 a.m. to 6
    p.m.

For this exercise, we shall decide on an ad size of 200 mm
(8 in) × 6 columns – at least half of which will be given over
to a list of carpet types and their respective prices. Which
means that the accompanying body copy must be reasonably short, relatively sharp and bang on target. No
extraneous guff. And there's no doubt that we require body
copy. How else can we put the delivery/estimate/planning
story across? A fast delivery statement, when you weigh it
up, is almost as important as the low-price message.

To start with, we require a headline. Several fairly
obvious lines suggest themselves immediately; and since
we are now working on copy rather than headlines, we'll
accept the first that come along. So:

MAGIC CARPETS.
AND A FLYING DELIVERY

Or, alternatively:

PILES OF CARPETS.
AND WALL-TO-WALL DISCOUNTS

Take your pick. Now the first step is to establish who and what we are talking about:

Walkover Carpets. The discount carpet store that gives you more for your money.
A lot more.

Followed by an outline of the USP:

Over 2000 carpet styles and patterns to choose from.
And all top-brand names. From as little as £2 a square yard.

And the availability story:

Either from stock. Or by our rush, 24-hour delivery service. Which, of course, comes absolutely free.

Reinforce the USP:

The widest possible choice at the lowest possible prices. Our bulk-buying policy takes care of that.

Now we cover the remaining selling points:

Free estimates. Free planning. Plus a next-day fitting service at very modest cost. And we're open 7 days a week 9 a.m. to 6 p.m.
Now cast your eyes over these unbeatable prices.

We might also include a 'flash' (a star-burst or balloon) containing the come-on:

(Flash)   *Ring for a no-obligation estimate – right now.*
Call: (Telephone)

As you can see, the copy developed quite naturally by:

1 Establishing the name of the firm and its business.
2 Clarifying, as soon as possible, the sentiments of the headline.
3 Introducing the peripheral services.
4 Urging the reader to take some positive action.

Additional points to note are that the USP is mentioned twice, and that sentences and paragraphs are tight and easy to scan.

All very straightforward. Nothing there to tax the mind of the average carpet buyer. And that's the whole point. The audience for this product is a wide mix of people across a broad band of the socio-economic spectrum. But what if your story is somewhat more complicated and your audience somewhat more concentrated?

You are, for instance, the manufacturer of a range of metal office-furniture. The products are made from a light, but tough alloy. Your key product, and the one you wish to promote, is an office desk which is specifically designed to carry computer hardware. These are the product details:

1 The desk – hereinafter called the Monitor – comes in a range of five sizes and six colour finishes.
2 It is built in such a way as to accept the various cable-kits, wires and leads so that they are neither visible nor inconvenient. All the wires can therefore be hidden within channels beneath the desk-top or within the drawers.
3 Thus, only the screen and keyboard are visible.
4 The Monitor is attractive and easy to maintain; and the computer hardware can be installed by any computer engineer.
5 Each desk is machine-finished with completely smooth edges and surfaces; and the drawers run on non-stick nylon gliders.

Your market is trade only i.e. office equipment suppliers. So the ad is to appear in business equipment publications.

Unquestionably, the USP is the fact that the desk is

designed to conceal unsightly wires and cables. Subsidiary sales points are the clean lines and good looks of the Monitor, along with the easy installations of the necessary hardware.

What about a headline, then? Something of the order of the following will probably do the trick:

IF YOU CAN'T TELL THE DIFFERENCE BETWEEN A COMPUTER DESK AND A NICE PIECE OF FURNITURE IT'S PROBABLY A MONITOR

Here, we would use a picture of the Monitor in an office reception area situation, complete with computer and screen – but not a cable in sight. Yet, because we are talking to the trade, shouldn't we be implying sales and profit? Like this:

WOULD YOU STAKE YOUR REPUTATION ON A COMPUTER DESK THAT DOESN'T HAVE ONE?

That's more like it – much more like it. And for this one we use the same picture as above. The copy is obviously geared towards the dealer who might stock our desks.

There are ordinary computer desks that make ordinary sales and profits.

And there are Monitor computer desks.

The desks that keep cable-kits and wires completely out of sight – all cleverly, but easily concealed. So the only thing you see is the computer.

Every Monitor desk is crammed with the sort of features that sales are made of.

- *Tough, high-grade alloy construction.*
- *Machine-finished, non-scratch surfaces.*
- *Simple computer installation and maintenance.*
- *Cables and leads are built right into the desk. So*

nothing shows – nothing gets in the way.
● *Non-stick, easy-glide nylon drawers.*

> *And behind each desk is the Monitor name.*
> *So before you stock an ordinary computer desk, ask yourself this.*
> *Can you afford to stake your reputation on a computer desk that doesn't have one?*
> *For all the facts and figures, please get in touch. And if you'd like a demonstration, we can arrange that, too.*
> *All you have to do is ask. Soon?*
> *Monitor* (logo)

I trust you see the difference between the two copy examples? The carpet copy just says it like it is – no frills – while the desk draft includes a little more persuasion. It's worth saying, too, that the entire desk ad revolves around its actual (or assumed) reputation. Well, reputation is relative; and even if your product is a fairly new one, of which very few people have even heard, it is a mistake not to endow it with an implied esteem. Always supposing, of course, that you have faith in it and are prepared to stand over the claims you make for it.

It so happens that I prefer persuasive copy – otherwise described as soft-sell copy – to any other kind. Hoop-la and razzmatazz are all right in their place; but soft-sell is all right in every place. This is a philosophy which has been hard learned over the years. In hindsight, I should have adopted it decades ago. Soft-sell is very effective; and where it can be used, it should be used. I now propose to demonstrate exactly what I mean.

I ask you to suppose that you are in the business of retailing computer equipment. Visualize, also, your position as the main distributor in your area for a particular make of computer – The Primrose. Fortunately, the manufacturer undertakes a high volume of national advertising and it could be fairly said that his is a household name. He also provides bundles of product literature, which you lose no time in putting into the hands of potential customers. From time to time, though, you are duty-bound to show your face in the media; if only to make sure that the market knows who you are, where you are, and what you sell. This being the case, you periodically run ads in the local press and local editions of business magazines. The definition of the market is businesses of all sizes, plus private individuals who desire a personal computer.

No doubt about it, these ads have no reason to scream and shout, or even raise their voices above a whisper, come to that. But they still have to sell; and they have to sell you – your professionalism, your service, your know-how.

To prepare such an ad, you will necessarily think 'self-assured'. You are nobody's mug; and you know your business inside out. When it comes to computers, nobody has more knowledge or technical acumen. Yet, without fear or favour, you are more than disposed to impart this knowledge to anyone who cares to ask for it. In the process, you will be sympathetic, understanding and, above all, genuinely helpful.

How to express these sentiments in a headline without sounding cocky? Indeed, how to do so in such a way that 'offer' and 'promise', while still inherent, are not rammed down the reader's throat? Like this perhaps:

OUR MOTTO: THE CUSTOMER
IS SOMETIMES WRONG

Continuing in the same vein, the body copy explains how we put the customer right.

Sometimes a customer will ask for one of our Primrose computer systems, or a Primrose personal computer. And we say 'no'. Regretfully but firmly.

The reason is simple. If the machine you want is not the machine you should have, we won't sell it to you. That's one of the ways we've built a reputation second-to-none in the computer business.

So before we talk computers, we talk problems.

Not just with you, but with the people who are going

to do the work-planning; the programming; and the operating.

You'll find that we ask a whole lot of questions – including the awkward ones.

But you'll find, too, that we come up with the answer. The right answer.

After all, isn't it worth spending an hour talking about something that's going to be working for you for years?

The Primrose brochure will show you what we do – and give you a good idea of how well we do it.

Please send for a copy. Or simply drop in.

We might, if we wished to expand this campaign, run a consecutive ad which offers a more or less identical message, but which talks to small companies in particular. A headline for it would say, in essence:

**ALL RIGHT: YOUR NAME ISN'T
ICI OR BARCLAYS.
DON'T LET THAT WORRY YOU**

Or, more reasonably:

**EVEN WHEN WE THINK SMALL,
WE THINK BIG**

The copy statement could then take this course:

Primrose computers are used by big-name companies like National Insurance, Harvey Wallbanger, Murder Incorporated and others.

But if yours is a medium-sized business or a small business, we'll take care of you, too.

Just as willingly and just as effectively.

With a range of computers and computer systems which all make the same simple promise . . . (Etc., etc.)

You may not be the biggest in your particular field.

**But that's no reason why you shouldn't have the best.
   Is it?**

And so on.

It's often a good idea in copy to mention the names of your clients, as I have done here – especially if they are big, or well regarded.

★   ★   ★

Weasel words

No doubt you've heard the above phrase used in radio and television programmes – usually derogatorily – when some poor advertising soul or other is being villified by an unctious interviewer about the rotten-to-the-core profession to which he misguidedly belongs.

To put it bluntly, weasel words are 'get-out' words. Words that destroy the force of a statement by equivocal qualification.

Contrary to popular belief, however, weasel words in copy are not designed to mislead – not by the true professional, anyway. Without wishing to flannel you, weasel words are there to protect the advertiser (or writer) from his competition and from the largely unwarranted attentions of a hardcore of the general public who make it their business to complain about anything and everything. These complaints can, at best, result in an expensive production being re-written or scrapped, or at worst, the prosecution of the advertiser.

Weasel words, then, are words such as:

'*Possibly* the finest floppy disk in the world.' Or: '*Almost certainly* the largest interior capacity *of any car of its kind.*' Or, again: '*We reckon it's the fastest delivery service, bar none.*'

When the manufacturer of a first-class product expresses a warrantable pride in it, in public, he must be very careful about what he says. Not because he may infringe the Trades Description Act 1968 – since that Act really only outlaws downright lies about the material content, or country of origin, or operating abilities, of a product. No, he has to watch his mouth on account of: (a) a competitor may jump up and show that his product is equally as good, which is as fine a way as any to lose a share of a market; or (b) the semi-pro complainers will put their oar into the long suffering Advertising Standards Authority people, who are obliged to investigate the complaint and who, however un-intentionally, put the wind up said advertiser and everyone connected with his publicity work.

Which is a great pity.

Of course, weasel words *are* sometimes used in less than candid ways – though I'd qualify that by saying they do not deliberately mislead. Generally, they induce the reader to draw a favourable conclusion about a product, to the detriment of similar products, but which all of the latter could quite properly claim for themselves if they had the wit.

Possibly the most famous of these is: *Nothing works faster than Anadin.* The fact that, in all probability, competing headache remedies work just as fast (given identical metabolic rates and digestive systems), is left unspoken. And if you wish to assume from this line that Anadin *works faster*, then so be it. But as a weasel, it's a cracker – and certainly 100 per cent better than the possible alternative: *One of the fastest headache remedies you can buy.*

Every time I see the Anadin line, however, I cannot but help grinning. If nothing works faster, then perhaps headache sufferers would be better off with nothing?

★　　★　　★

Sales letters and mailers

In your advertising scheme of things, you may find it expedient to prepare sales letters and mailing shots. These should be written, as near as makes no difference in the same style as the copy you use for your ads. To put it briefly:

1   Make your point immediately.
2   Firm up on the message with a few well-chosen words.
3   Close with an enjoiner to find out more.

Whatever you do, stay away from long, tortuous sentences – they will not be read.

I must be one of the very few people who reads every item of sales mail that comes through the door. I do so because I like to see what others are up to. Some of this material is exceptional in its presentation and content, but a lot of it is, as the man said, junk. Badly written, badly presented and hardly calculated to have me leaping out of my chair to find out more.

I often wonder why people go to all the time, trouble and cost of typing/printing and postage. Indeed, I regularly contemplate what it must be like for the senders of the offending material and experience a twinge of pity. I picture them in their small, dingy offices eagerly awaiting a response that never materializes.

Did I say small and dingy offices? Yes, I did; because all the evidence which decants through my letterbox clearly shows that it is the smaller firms who are responsible for producing the bulk of the garbage mentioned. This could be – and doubtless is – blamed on the lack of funds; but seven times out of ten, no money in the world could salvage it, or prevent it from coming as such a crushing anti-climax. The writers not only have no basic understanding of how to put a sales letter together, but have seemingly taken no trouble to find out. I should be much more impressed by a letter written by someone who has at least put himself out to communicate with me in a way that doesn't put my back up or prompt me to doubt his propositions. Any old thing will do, they seem to say. That's near enough for jazz, they mock. Well, it patently isn't.

I have in my hand a mailer (for the sake of clarity, I shall put letters and printed mail-shots under the 'mailer' heading) from a smallish local firm telling me that it manufactures and sells wrought iron garden furniture.

'*Dear Sir,*' it begins; but even I won't argue with that. '*You will be glad to note that this company now has available a full range of exquisite garden furniture,*' it continues. Oh, will I? I reply. On what, pray, do you base that assumption?

Why *presume* in this manner and beg the inevitable question? Daft, I call it.

Mailers containing such statements as: '*You will be delighted to learn,*' Or: '*We know you can't wait to see,*' assume that we are all busting a gut to be sold something. And in this assumption they are making an egregious error. The indisputable fact is that 99.9 per cent of us aren't.

I advocate directness, but directness applied to the product or service on offer – certainly never to what the writer *supposes* the reader may think. You are soliciting somebody from a distance; you cannot possibly begin to know what a prospect believes or holds dear.

In which case, don't try.

On the other hand, those with an opening gambit like: '*We are immensely proud to bring to your attention,*' And: '*We would ask you to do us the kindness of perusing,*' carry all the artificial humbleness of a Uriah Heep and, as such, make the reader wilt in his boots (or, not to offend any of my more sensitive readers, male or female, his stilettos).

Another fault with mailer copy – and with ad copy, too, come to that – is the disturbing practice of posing a question in the opening line. (I am not, most definitely not, referring to the interrogative in headlines; that's an entirely different matter.) The defaulters I'm alluding to kick the copy off in such a way that anything more contrived would be hard to imagine. They go something like this: '*Haven't you always wished you could enjoy the luxury of a full-size sunbed in your own home? Well now you can.*' Or: '*Have you noticed how so many women are using Set-Rite Shampoo these days – instead of ordinary, non-nourishing hair preparations? Well they are.*'

This, to my mind, is not clever. Because as sure as night follows day, the immediate response from the majority of your audience – whether consciously or not – is bound to be: '*No, as a matter of fact I haven't.*'

What should mailer copy look like? As I've said, it should very much reflect your ad copy; and as for sales letters, specifically, cast your eyes over the following – a brief solicitation from an office cleaning company to a prospective customer.

> **Dear Mister Boat,**
> **This Company has been in the office cleaning business for five years.**
>
> **Long enough to know that customers shouldn't have to put up with second best. Long enough to know that in the long run, efficiency and pride in a job well done are just as important as making a profit.**
>
> **Our customers like it that way.**
>
> **If you'd care to know how we can put some sparkle into your office premises. Make it a pleasure to visit and work in. All for very modest cost. Please complete the reply-paid card.**
>
> **Alternatively, you may prefer to give us a ring.**
>
> **Either way, we'll be glad to show you exactly what our well-trained staff and modern equipment can do. And who we already do it for.**
>
> **We think you'll be agreeably surprised.**
>
> **Most sincerely,**
>
> **Roland Butter**

This letter doesn't set out to sell in the strictest sense. All it wishes to achieve is the implanting in the mind of the reader the basic facts (a) that the company exists, (b) what it exists for, (c) its availability.

Any follow-up letter – and you should always be ready with a follow-up, since a series of mailings will act as a memory-jogger and is more likely to cue the prospect into taking some action – would probably say something after the manner of. 'Since our last letter, we have won several new clients, and here's a list of the companies we work for – along with brief details of the range of services we offer.'

Likewise, a series of tightly-worded letters will stand more chance of being read than a single mailer running to several turgid pages.

On the pure mailer side of things – the specially printed presentation – one can spend thousands of pounds. But if you keep your ideas simple (and simple ideas can be just as attractive and effective) you will in turn keep your expenditure low.

To illustrate what I mean, there is a UK company that specializes in printing up to five colours on all types of envelope stock – from manilla to cream wove, and everything in between. Which is a neat trick if you can do it, because envelopes aren't the easiest of materials to print on. What's more, getting the colours to register (exactly correspond in position to each other) on material of such varying substance is no mean feat. Nevertheless, they can do it.

Normally, to achieve his promotional aims, a printer will simply run off some samples of work he has done for others and use these as publicity material. But this is not greatly imaginative, so the firm in question approached an advertising agency and requested some bright ideas for promoting the service.

In due course, said agency came back with a splendid rough of a mailer which was, in essence, a folder containing a series of envelope and letterhead designs. Now, on these were printed the totally chimerical logos/trading symbols of five well-known characters from fact and fiction. As I remember it, among the characters were The Invisible Man (printed black and white), Julius Caesar (two colours), right up to Michelangelo (five colours).

The mailer showed, very graphically, that the company was, indeed, capable of printing envelopes in five colours and, without the slightest doubt, could do so for just about anybody.

You will realize that the letterheads were included mainly for effect; but they were given a subsidiary function in that each letterhead sheet carried a typed letter, supposedly from the character concerned.

Which was where I came in.

For the fun of it, I include a King Arthur letter, which was part of the presentation, and I ask you to visualize a logo at the head of it consisting of a circular device, not unlike the legendary Round Table, inside which is a female hand brandishing Excalibur.

Lady Guinevere
c/o The Round Table
Glastonbury

My Dearest Guinevere,
Just a short note to tell you that we are still clanking around in the woods looking for wrongs to right, fiery dragons to slay and damsels to distress. I only hope that Government subsidy comes through soon, so that we can put some *real* professionals on to this job. I'm toying with the idea of calling them social workers.

Merlin has been up to his old tricks again. Yesterday, he turned a bishop into a castle, a knight into a pawnshop, and checkmated a couple of queens.

Incidentally, how does the four-colour Round Table symbol on the envelope grab you? Pretty good, eh? Specially, when you realize that printing hasn't been invented yet.

But enough of me. Is Lancelot taking good care of you? I hope he's not getting under your feet, or into your hair – or anywhere else come to that. (Fie! I must be jousting.) Shall have to have a word with that boy. He's getting too big for his sabatons, I feel.
Well, must close.

Your loving legend,

Arthur (King)

In this instance, quite obviously, the mailer cost the printer virtually nothing except time and a modest artwork charge. Even so, a similar exercise would cost the average businessman in the street a lot less than, say, a full-blown, full-colour mailer. But purely as an example, it shows that mailers don't have to be complicated affairs. Clever use of tints, for instance, can turn an ordinary black-and-white mailer/brochure into a production that hits the eye like a two-colour job. Further, two-colour work treated in the same manner can be made to look like three colours. And so on.

I hope to prove the point more convincingly later on in the book.

Stick around.

★   ★   ★

Radio scripting

To crack the essence of scripting, we may once again be wise to dream up a hypothetical marketing situation and try to fulfil it with a decent commercial. For this exercise, let's take a product that's different in every respect from what we've used so far – and one that's possibly a lot closer to your heart.

A pub. A pub called the Don Quixote in Victoria Street.

This establishment is situated on the edge of a large town and, because of that, is in competition with several hundred other pubs. As part and parcel of this tavern's premises there is a large hall which, in the past, the management (you) has tried to market successively (but by no means successfully) as a business conference locale, a banqueting hall and a venue for wedding receptions. All, as I say, to little avail. Now, in your wisdom, you have decided to flog it as a jazz centre – a place where several hundred aficionados can sit back, *drink*, and enjoy the music of both a resident band and specially invited, out-of-town groups and vocalists. The kind of music you will be featuring is 1950s/1960s 'modern' jazz, which is still played to great effect by many British combos. Accordingly, you have refurbished the hall, decorated it with pictures of famous jazz musicians, musical instruments, record album sleeves, and such.

After much thought, you have christened the place Jazz City. You'll be open for business every evening and on Saturday lunchtime.

Our priority, it seems to me, is to get the name and purpose of the venue across with some immediacy. Though we have to do so in a way that appeals to jazz-lovers; and also in such a way as to make it appear that we have a more than passing acquaintance with that brand of music.

With regard to the name-promulgation part of the process, there used to be (and still is in some misguided quarters) a practically universal belief that if the company or product wasn't mentioned by name on at least six separate occasions in a commercial, said commercial showed all the symptoms of a failure and was sure to be a flop.

This was, and remains, nothing short of utter claptrap. If only because I have personally discovered that repetition of this nature (unentertaining, non-amusing repetition) never achieves its intended aim – that of implanting the name firmly in the mind of the listener. In reality, it has quite the opposite effect. The listener switches off; and he very often does so physically as well as mentally.

Normally, when I pass an adverse – or, as in this case, a semi-adverse – opinion on other people's efforts, it is accepted with a good deal of unruffled calm. Few blood-vessels are burst and few horse-whippings threatened. The odd protest, disclaimer or rebuff may come from an affronted advertiser or ad agency; but in general the volume of disapproval is seldom such as to put any undue pressure on our law enforcement agencies.

In this case, however, things are different. Because when I happened to air this view about name repetition recently to a group of advertising people, I received what was, relatively speaking, a whole basketful of objections. And from the tone of them, I was the basket.

Their argument could be summed up like this: 'Identification of the advertiser is the single most important ingredient of a commercial.'

Well, I couldn't agree more; and I'm all for it – but not in the way they suggest. Not by ramming it incessantly down the audience's throat. So however strident the volume of disagreement, I continue to hold to my belief: that a commercial should strive to be so interesting, so entertaining to the listener, that he will, as a matter of course, listen out for 'who it's for'. In which case, a couple of mentions of the product name or service title is most certainly sufficient.

There are, of course, exceptions to this general rule. The launch of a new product, for instance, will cry out for plenty of 'naming'; and certain script scenarios revolve almost entirely around the name. One that springs to mind is the Martini commercial of many years ago which ran on radio throughout the United States. The set-up was a husband and wife in a bar discussing the various implications of the Martini name. 'They're obviously Italians, Wilbur,' says she.

'Although, Hon,' replies the man, 'Martini is an anagram of Ian Trim. So they could be Scotch,' or words to that effect.

And it goes on. But the pay-off is a classic.

'Well, whatever these Martini people are, sweetheart – *they sure make great ashtrays.*'

If that commercial didn't win every advertising award going, there is something very wrong somewhere.

But I digress; let's get back to Jazz City.

Our final consideration is the reason we are doing all this. To encourage people to visit the establishment and spend money on booze. Clearly, the ITCA would have a massive coronary if we were to put it as baldly as that. We are, therefore, obliged to go canny; and the alcohol content of our commercial will necessarily be barely measurable.

So let's do it. I recommend a male voice-over with an American drawl. Better than that, it ought to be one of those superb, dark-brown, East Coast voices and delivered with all the jive of a resident of Harlem.

Where will you find one? You almost certainly won't; but I reckon a versatile professional voice could make a pretty authentic stab at it. I'd also suggest some library music in the shape of a slow-tempo piano as a background to the voice.

The length of the commercial? How about 40 seconds. And like this:

Jazz City	40-second radio
Male voice over: (Cool, laid back 'jive' delivery.)	'You dig Gillespie, man? Coltraine? Canonball Aderlay?
SFX: Sound effects Slow-tempo jazz piano.	You go for the sweet sounds of Art Pepper – or the jump-right-on-it of Lester Young . . . ?
	Well, I guess you've come to the right place. I'm saying Jazz City, man. At the Don Quixote in Victoria Street.
	Where the beer is cool; and the jazz is like fri-gid-air. Live music, cosy company, and wall-to-wall jazz . . .
	Jazz City. Where every night is jazz night – and Saturday lunchtime, too.
	It's in Victoria Street . . . you dig?'

That ought to do the trick fairly well. It says everything we want to say; and it seems to have the right tone for the audience. If you read it at a slowish pace, it fits the forty seconds with ease. Note the pauses, indicated by the three-dot ellipses. These would be filled, as you'll realize, by the backing music – which should be upfaded and downfaded within the breaks. The pauses, I might add, are as material to a radio commerical as are the words themselves. They give full emphasis to what has gone before by allowing it time to sink in.

Radio is a sound medium; so use sound – and that includes silences. An unbearable pause is a superb ear-pricker.

For effect, the above commercial should begin with a few bars of the piano music as an introduction to the voice. Thereafter, it will run under. A conscientious engineer will also try to time the voice to finish close to the end of a musical phrase, thus giving the piece a neat finale. Failing that, he'd probably recommend a slow fade on the music. Another ploy is to start the music at the appropriate number of seconds from the end of the tune – in this case it's forty. Like that, you can be sure of a natural ending, a buttoned-up ending, to the spot.

I've already spoken about writing specifically for well-known voices, but further debate is in order. The secret of success here is to study the personality in much the same way as an impressionist must. Listen carefully to his or her normal pace of delivery; latch on to key words; examine the typical phrasing, inflection and construction of sentences; gauge the pauses and, probably most importantly of all, retain their voice in your mind as you write the piece.

To clarify things, I reproduce two completely different 30-second scripts, for two entirely different personalities, which I wrote a year or two back. The first, featuring the remarkable voice of Vincent Price, is for the London Dungeon. (Should you not be familiar with this establishment it is, in principle, a waxworks that majors on British mediaeval history. It's all rather gory, too.) The second script aims to promote an ice show at Wembley arena and uses the voice of the amazingly articulate Terry Wogan.

Both commercials are targeted at more or less identical audiences: family parties, in the main, and youngsters via mums and dads in particular.

The striking aspect of the scripts is that the wordage is roughly the same amount for both. And that is surprising, since one might suspect that Mr Price has a *far* slower delivery than Mr Wogan. The difference, in fact, is six or seven words over the thirty seconds – not that much slower at all.

Here they are:

The London Dungeon   30-second radio

SFX: Hollow footsteps – run under throughout

MVO:
(Vincent Price)

'I've made some horrific movies in my time – but I've just witnessed probably the most devilish scenario ever to come my way.

I refer, of course, to the London Dungeon . . . here, in dank vaults beneath London Bridge.

The London Dungeon, you see, presents British mediaeval history in all its more gruesome aspects. And it does so deliciously . . . exquisitely.

Tortures, hangings, decapitations, demonology and witchcraft.

A truly splendid day out for any boy and ghoul.

SFX: Slight echo on voice   I'll stake your heart on it.'

Wembley Arena   30-second radio

SFX: Bolero-type music off-mike
      Echo a la the interior of an arena

MVO:
(Terry Wogan)

Right – get your skates on, we're all going for a holiday on ice.

Oh, yes, we are.

Because *Holiday on Ice* is a smashing new family show that opens December 27th at the good old Wembley Arena.

It's a programme absolutely jam-packed with glittering spectacle and breathtaking action. Not to mention a multiplicity of beautiful young ladies – oh, so scantily clad.

That'll steam your glasses up, grandad.

Holiday on Ice. From December 27th. Tickets from Wembley Arena or good agents . . .'

SFX: MVO moving off-mike

'Ok, girls – I'll show you that double-axle just once more.'

I think we've explored the writing aspect of advertising pretty thoroughly, don't you? Not that I think for one moment the subject could ever be exhausted. But as a guideline, it's as complete as I would care to make it in a book of this nature. And I certainly don't expect you to hurry away and start penning volumes of advertising material simply for the thrill of it. Always supposing I've acquitted myself, though, I do expect you to have a better grasp of what goes into the writing of an ad or a commercial than you did when we started. The mental somersaults and the verbal gymnastics.

You have? Oh, thank the Lord for that. I thought for a moment you were about to demand your money back.

Anyway, I hope I have said nothing which will in any way prevent you from committing advertising.

9 Devising cost-effective promotions

This, folks, is the bit you've all been waiting for. The bit where you can sit back, relax, adopt pipe, slippers, feather boa, or see-through nightie, according to your predilection, and observe with any degree of enthusiasm you so wish the promotional ideas I have devised, resurrected and re-hashed to your considerable benefit and, I shouldn't wonder, eternal gratitude.

My intention is to present a whole wadge of ideas which may either be used 'as is', or suitably adjusted. All you will have to do, therefore, is present the words and pictures to your printer or publications ad manager and he will have it set, not to music as it so patently deserves, but in type and illustration. (Just tell him I sent you.) Similarly, you will be able to use the background to each promotion as an administrative and tactical guide.

I hope.

As we work through this lot, I shall reproduce rough layouts and appropriate copy for each idea. Plus roughs and copy for ads where necessary – along with any PR material you may need.

★   ★   ★

When the general public thinks of sales promotions, if it thinks of them at all, its first and immediate reaction is to point to the national scratch-card and petrol voucher schemes of the likes of Shell and Esso or, maybe the big-prize competitions launched by *Readers Digest* and various mail-order houses.

Considering the vast amount of money which is spent on them, it is a natural enough reaction.

What they don't realize, or perhaps don't care to realize, is that they are being 'got at' by literally thousands of promotional gambits every day in the UK. These are, in the main, ephemeral and localized one-offs produced by small companies but which, in their own way, can produce even better results than the major national operations.

Someone once said that everything is relative – which, when you think about it, it very probably is. So what is the better business proposition – investing £2,000 to recoup £10,000 in increased sales, or spending £2,000,000 to make £10,000,000?

I dare say, the £10,000 is far more valuable to the small businessman than the £10,000,000 is to the conglomerate. Because in 'doing it himself', in being the prime-mover behind the campaign, the small businessman has no palms to grease, no promotions executives to support, and no 15 per cent being creamed off the top by high-flying promotions houses.

What is a promotion? Generally speaking, it's any gambit which grabs the attentions of potential customers forcibly enough to prompt them to patronize you at the expense of others. Anything from a simple mailing that offers goods at specially reduced prices, to a consumer competition with prizes as the end result, but with customer 'traffic' through your store or showroom as the motive.

★   ★   ★

Warning: competitions can seriously damage your wealth

Before you run any kind of consumer competition, take care to read the chapter and verse of the Gaming Act and any of its possible amendments. (You can pick up copies from Her Majesty's Stationery Office.) I say take care, because you could end up on the wrong side of the revenue men and find yourself hauled into court; and that could prove expensive.

The problem with consumer competitions – and the essence of the Act – is this. Any competition which relies on proof of purchase for entry, must contain within the structure of the competition an *element of skill*. In other words, where you ask punters to buy your product as a condition of their taking part in a competition, you cannot operate a draw in which luck-of-the-draw determines the winner. Straight prize draws can only be mounted where no product purchase is involved. Neither can you, for instance, conceal a winning number (or symbol) within a product, then announce that anyone who buys the particular product with the number on it wins a trip to Portugal, or some such. Here, the winner is determined by pure chance – no skill on the part of the entrant is involved. Hence, it's illegal. So, in cases like this, you must build an element of skill into the competition to stay on the right side of the law.

Patently, though, a competition calling for too much skill (or knowledge) will be quickly by-passed by customers. They mostly have neither the time, nous or energy to solve complicated puzzles and quizzes.

The way around it is to run a competition which is so simple to complete that even the fourth-form idiot can do it – but *include*, within the bones of the competition, *a tie-breaker*. You know the sort of thing I mean. Include a phrase which says something to the effect of: *Using your skill and judgement, complete the following sentence in no more than 10 words. 'I buy Pretty Boy budgie seed because . . .'*

That as far as the law-makers are concerned, represents the necessary element of skill and is, to all intents and purposes, the device by which you arrive at the winner of your competition.

It's potty, I know. Because the main thrust of the competition – the 'is this the Eiffel Tower, Tower Bridge, or the Leaning Tower of Pisa?' bit – is more or less redundant, since it's now so easy that 99 per cent of the competitors will get it right.

Nevertheless, these are roughly the rules, so stick to them.

With regard to competitions aimed, as it were, at the trade, i.e. at firms' buyers, for example, the law is not so particular. A competition whose motive is to coerce companies into buying more of your product – and where a purchase has to be made in order to enter – the skill component is unnecessary. Presumably, the law-makers reckon that businesses need less protection than the solitary consumer; and maybe they're right.

But there's an anomaly, here. Firms' buyers, by definition, are generally intelligent people who know that the odds against winning a straight draw can be hundreds, thousands or even millions to one. In which case, they would rather take part in a competition where skill or knowledge is the arbiter. It's a paradox that really doesn't need further explanation.

★   ★   ★

To open, we'll first look at a few fundamental mailer promotions and how they operate.

Mailer 1

Give us a ring – we'll even pay for the call

You are a soft-furnishing retailer. In your neighbourhood are thirty hotels and guesthouses whose business you could well do with.

Put together thirty packs consisting of:

1 A short letter on your own letterhead (a) outlining the quality of your goods and services, (b) mentioning any percentage reductions/discounts you may be offering, and (c) asking the prospect to pick up the phone and give you a call.
2 A polythene envelope containing a *brand-new* 10p coin.
3 A sample sheaf of fabrics (curtains, seat covering, etc.), but only if you are offering reductions on these. And make the samples compact enough to go through the post.

4   A neatly typed list of prices – keying discount prices to
    fabrics if these are included.

Put the whole lot in a simple folder or spine-binder.
Alternatively, have a wallet specially printed. The unit cost
of all this shouldn't come to more than around £2 –
including postage. At a profit margin of 33⅓ per cent, you
need pull only one order of £180 to break even. But,
whatever happens, you have put a foot in the door of thirty
new customers. In the unlikely event that nobody calls, you
can either send a follow-up letter that says: '*Don't call us,
we'll call you,*' and then call, or phone within three or four
days of sending the first mailer.

This very basic promotion can be utilized by a variety of
small businesses. I've seen it operated effectively by a
garage proprietor who wished to remind previous customers that the car they bought last year is now a year old,
and isn't it about time they thought of changing it? '*So give
us a ring –we'll give you a better-than-average trade-in price on
your current car,*' was the come-on.

For reasons that are quite beyond me, since I'm no
psychologist, the 10p bit works a lot harder than its face
value would suggest. Seemingly, people are decent enough
not to take the money and run. They feel obliged to make a
gesture of some kind – even if it's thanks, but no thanks.

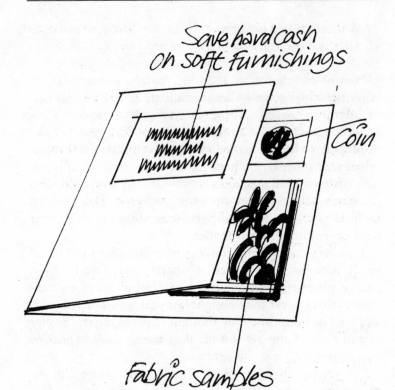

Figure 3

Folder label:

SAVE HARD CASH
ON SOFT FURNISHINGS

Give us a ring – we'll even pay for the call.

Letter copy:
Dear Mr X,
Nowadays, most soft furnishing costs are pretty
good. But ours happen to be that much better.
    And the accompanying price-list proves the
point. One good reason, perhaps, for you to take
advantage of our special soft furnishing contract
rates.

We can provide everything from a glass-cloth to the re-upholstery of bar seating. From bath mats to curtains. From continental quilts to shower curtains.

Everything you need, in fact, for the coming summer season. At prices you can live with.

We make no charge for estimates; and we're happy to travel anywhere, anytime, to talk things over.

All you have to do is ask. And we enclosed the cost of the call, for that very purpose.

Do it now – why don't you?

Sincerely,

Mailers in the same vein, but not quite, are the following:

Mailer 2

How to nail down a decent joiner
An ordinary 4 in nail attached to a pre-printed card. Plus relevant copy. (Would it be possible to have the phone number engraved on the nail?) The mailer can be aimed at the householder or the builder.

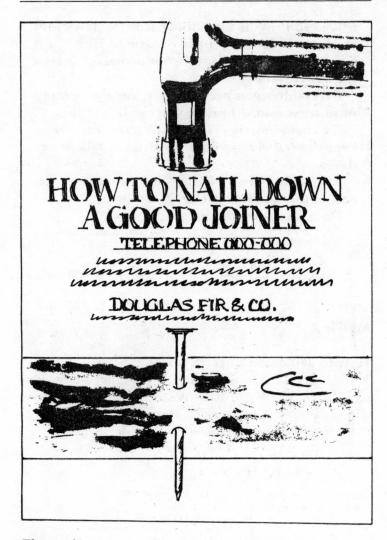

Figure 4

Copy:
(Telephone number)
When you need a good joiner, here's the number to ring.
- ● **For contract work – first and second fixing.**
- ● **For kitchen unit installation. Stud-work and partitioning.**

- And for house extensions, alterations and renovation work.

(Company name and address)

Mailer 3

How to flush out a good plumber

A rubber or fibre washer stuck to a pre-printed card. The washer therefore becomes part of the headline. Plus copy.

Figure 5

Copy:
(Telephone number)
We are jobbing plumbers. So we can handle anything from a burst pipe to putting a washer on a tap.

Better still, we'll install complete bathroom suites, or re-plumb a home.

And if you need central heating (solid fuel, gas or oil) just call this number.

We'll give you a free, no quibble quotation.

(Company name and address)

Mailer 4

How to get wired into a reliable electrician
Two short lengths of wire, the ends exposed, are stuck on a pre-printed card. The telephone number appears in the gap. (Copy would be similar in tone to Mailers 2 and 3 above.)

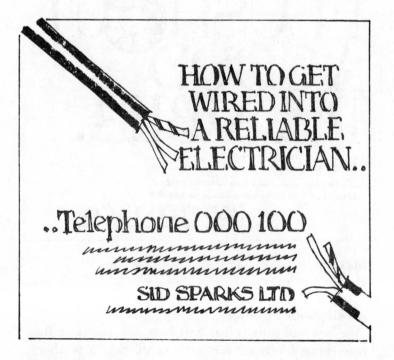

Figure 6

Mailer 5

Look what we've taken off our carpets

A small square of carpet stuck on a pre-printed card. To be aimed at those builders who carpet their newly built homes, or at hotels direct.

Figure 7

Copy:
Make no mistake. This carpet offer is for carpets cheap. Not cheap carpets.

Just for the offer, we've taken a full X% off the price of every carpet in our vast range.

So you can now buy Royal Wilton for only £X a square yard. Cosset from £X. Or bottom of the range Chalfont for as little as £X.

What's more, we'll also give you an extra X% discount for orders totalling more than XXX square yards.

You can find out more by calling us now.

(Company name and address)

Mailer 6

Here's one book you won't mind catching your secretary reading

You are in the office equipment business and you want to get a variety of branded-product leaflets into the hands of office managers.

Have a simple folder printed – with the line given above, plus your name and address, of course – and enclose the leaflets.

An alternative cover line is:

THIS IS ONE OF OUR MOST SUCCESSFUL PRODUCTS.
IT'S YOURS – FREE

A covering letter says that you only make the folders. But the leaflets contained therein are from some of the biggest office-equipment manufacturers in the world. And, right now, you're offering some worthwhile discounts on all of them.

Mailer 7

Servicing checklist

Here's an extremely simple and inexpensive idea for any company offering a regular servicing/maintenance service to other businesses. Attach a cheap biro – with your name engraved – to a pre-printed card.

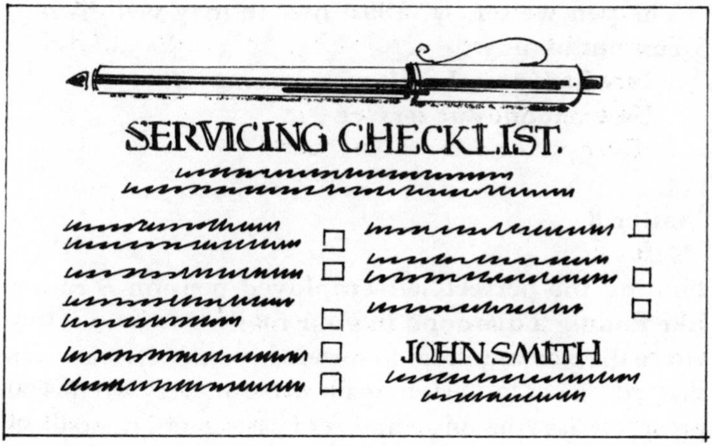

Figure 8

The principle of it is an opening statement such as:

Does your garage/office cleaning service etc., give you the kind of service you deserve?

This is followed by a series of sales points. 'Do you get a two-hour turn round?' Or: 'Are they on call 24 hours?', with yes/no tick boxes.

The final lines says:

If you've answered NO to more than four questions, maybe you should give us a call. Because our service is YES all the way.

It's unlikely that anyone will bother to tick the boxes, but they will almost certainly pocket your biro. Which is a good enough way to keep your name in front of them.

With continuity in mind, you may care to wait a few weeks, then send out another pen – along with a short message thus:

The pen we sent you last month may well have run out by now.

In which case, here's a replacement.

Now, about our service . . .

Mailer 8

Finding the perfect self-employed pension is rather like finding a diamond in your mail

Given that you can afford to spend a little money, and given that you have located a small group of very promising prospects, lash out on a number of paste gems, rhinestones or marcasites and mount one on the inside front cover of each four-page mailer.

FINDING THE
PERFECT SELF EMPLOYED
PENSION
IS RATHER LIKE
FINDING A
DIAMOND IN YOUR MAIL.

Figure 9

The inside cover says:

UNTIL NOW, IT COULDN'T BE DONE WITH ANY
REAL HOPE OF SUCCESS

While page three reads:

WE'D LIKE TO TALK TO YOU ABOUT A FLAWLESS PENSION PLAN FOR THE SELF-EMPLOYED

Figure 10

Along with copy:

We are sole agents for Superstar Insurance.

   The company which has developed a self-employed pension plan that really does give you more.

- **A lump sum of £XXX,XXX on retirement.**
- **Plus a monthly pension of £XXX.XX.**
- **With free £XX a week accident cover.**
- **All for an annual premium of £XX.**

Obviously, you don't have to be an insurance agent to utilize this idea. Suitably re-worded, it will work for just about anybody. As an example, let's assume you're a computer products retailer with an agency for a certain make of floppy disk. In which case the cover would read:

FINDING THE PERFECT FLOPPY DISK IS RATHER LIKE FINDING A DIAMOND IN YOUR MAIL

And the inside would look something like this:

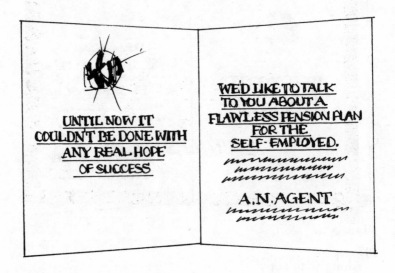

Figure 11

Mailer 9

Here's a four-page mail-shot for a clothing manufacturer who needs to make new contacts in the retail trade. It would even work for a hairdresser or, dare I say it, a public relations company.

O WAD SOME POW'R THE GIFTIE GIE US TO SEE OURSELVES AS OTHERS SEE US

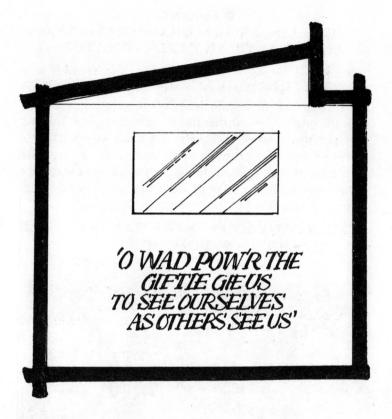

Figure 12

It's an oblong of silver foil (silver faced card) stuck to the mailer. The inside would contain the relevant sales details.

Mailer 10

Some mailers arrive looking like mailers. Don't ask me why, they just do. When this happens, they stand a very good chance of going straight into the waste-bucket unopened.

How to avoid this happening? What about a printed sticker to go on the envelope.

WARNING:
THIS PLAIN, BROWN WRAPPER CONTAINS
MATERIAL OF AN EXPLICIT NATURE.

Which, of course, it does – seeing as how it holds your product literature. The chances of it being opened in a hurry are, I would say, not so much a fair bet as a racing certainty.

In the unlikely event that none of the foregoing rewards you with the response you need, here's a shake-up mailer to jog memories and promote some action. It's a card (half A5), printed both sides. Side 1 is a reversed-out illustration (white out of solid black) of a spiritualist's table or ouija board, accompanied by the reversed-out message:

IS THERE ANYBODY THERE WANTS TO TALK TO ANYBODY HERE?

Figure 13

Side 2 should contain a precis of the message you have sent previously. Maybe a headline such as the following might do the trick:

WE'VE TRIED WRITING.
WE'VE EVEN TRIED ESP.
BUT THIS WAS THE ONLY WAY WE COULD
REACH YOU.

Perhaps it's time we looked at promotions proper. Why not?

Promo 1

Find the gold star

Any retailer, garage, supermarket or record shop can mount this easy-to-operate promotion at nominal cost.

To open, run a short series of uncomplicated ads which announce your intention of giving away a prize of goods or cash to the person who finds a gold star (it's a gold-coloured sticker about the size of a 10p piece) which is located somewhere in your store or showroom.

You can build an announcement into your window-display, and place reminders at strategic points within the premises prior to the event.

The gold star in question is attached, not-so-conspicuously, to one of your products. Customers will therefore have to explore the place pretty thoroughly in order to find it. Which means that if you and your sales assistants are on your toes, the additional shop-traffic can be put to profitable advantage. (As an extension of the promotion, you may wish to include both a silver and a blue star and offer extra prizes.)

Have a photographer on standby to capture the finder – possibly with yourself in the picture, smilingly handing over the prize. These shots can be employed for subsequent window displays and for release to the local press. Try to organize the pictures outside the shop, where your frontage can be identified.

Typical ad:

FIND THE GOLD STAR
AND WIN £100 CASH

(Picture of solid black star of identical size to the gold star)

Drop into our XXXXXX Street store this coming Wednesday – and the visit could make you £100 the richer.

All you have to do is look around our various displays and find a gold star located somewhere in the store.

It's about the size of the one shown above.

When you've found it, take it along to one of our assistants and the £100 is *yours*.

You don't have to buy anything. So you've nothing to lose and £100 to win.

That's Wednesday, XXth August. See you then?

(Company name and address)

The PR opportunities with this one are quite substantial. Be certain to tell the ad manager of your local paper that you are taking space on the condition that he publishes a picture and/or report of the event. Check with him, too, the latest time you can submit your photographs for early publication.

Promo 2

Used car Dutch auction

Now and again, a car-dealer will find himself swamped by a showroomful of used cars. This often occurs after the launch of a new car, or when a new registration comes into force. Come to think of it, it almost always occurs; and the poor old dealer is up to his hocks in used vehicles which he not only doesn't want, but which take up valuable space that could be more profitably employed housing new cars.

How to clear the showroom? One way is like this:

Run a single ad for three or four consecutive days before the *weekend* of the promotion. The 'auction' must be staged throughout a Saturday and Sunday to ensure pulling the optimum amount of interest and traffic.

This ad will list the used vehicles you want to shift, plus their 'starting prices'. In the headline of the ad, you state that each of these vehicles will be reduced in price by £20 (or whatever the mathematics suggest) every hour, on the hour – during your opening hours – starting 9 a.m. Saturday and finishing at 6 p.m. on Sunday.

The initial pricing of the cars is, without question, a most important consideration. Any car which runs the full gamut of time is going to lose £360 at the £20 rate given. But whatever the overall loading you build-in to cover the cost of the operation, the cars must be seen to be bargains. Otherwise, the promotion won't get past first base. Clearly, this calls for several 'loss leaders' – a few cars offered at well below their real value, so as to attract potential customers into the scheme and into your show-room – plus a judicious buying-in policy which allows a substantial and realistic mark-up on the remainder.

As the auction hours go by, then, you update the vehicle prices by changing the windscreen-sticker prices on each. This should be done with some efficiency and, I would add, not without a touch of showmanship.

Now it might be argued that customers will hold back until the last possible moment before making a purchase, with the obvious intention of getting the best possible deal. Not so. If they have their minds firmly set on a particular vehicle, just how long can they reasonably wait before it is sold right under their noses? It goes without saying that you and your salespeople will be doing everything to foster their apprehension.

I have used this promotion to great effect over the years; and I have, on one or two occasions, seen it completely clear showrooms of everything on four wheels – including cars which weren't even in the auction.

The promotion can, of course, be easily adapted to work in other areas – electrical goods; radios; televisions; fridges; and even furniture.

The very unsophisticated ad runs:

SAVE UP TO
£360
IN OUR USED CAR
DUTCH AUCTION

Here's your chance to save a lot of money on a first-class used car.

Up to £360, in fact.

Because we're reducing the price of all these cars by £20 every hour, on the hour.★

From 9 a.m. Saturday XXth to 6 p.m. Sunday XXth October.

So if you're in the market for a bargain, you'd better drop in and keep tabs on the action.

And as soon as we reach the price you want to pay, stake your claim – fast. Before someone else does.

While you're here, we'll provide tea, coffee and sandwiches. Plus balloons and badges for the youngsters.

Now take a careful look at the cars and their starting prices.

(List of cars, along with prices)

(Company name and address)

★ During our opening hours.

Figure 14

Promo 3

Staff silhouettes

You run a supermarket or a general retail store, and have a staff of ten or more. Because of fierce local competition, you desperately need to find some way of drawing people into your domain. Once there, you're convinced that the quality of your merchandise and the standard of service will convert them into regular customers.

Say no more. Have a photographer take individual profile shots of half-a-dozen of your sales staff and instruct him to turn them into solid black silhouettes of about 38 mm by 50 mm. Alternatively, ask an artist to produce simple caricatures. These are then incorporated in a competition entry form – which will be available at the entrance to your store. (In addition, you could produce large blow-ups of the silhouettes or caricatures and incorporate them in a window-display.)

What the customer has to do is identify those members of the staff featured in the entry form, and write his or her name below each representation. To assist them, your staff will be wearing large name-tags for easy identification. The entry form is then completed and deposited in a collection box at the door or checkout. Thereafter, all the forms go into a draw and the winner determined.

I reckon the finest prize a supermarket can offer in these circumstances is a trolleyful of groceries, i.e. as much product as the winner can cram into a trolley and wheel to the checkout for tallying. (You'll need to know how much you're giving away.) In the event, it would be a more than clever gesture – since the winner is odds on to be a woman – to have a hefty male assistant standing by, ready to jump in and offer his services for the pushing chore. And don't forget to get a photograph of it, either. Second and third prizes, if you wish to implement them, could be 'a basketful' of groceries.

Press advertising back-up to the promotion is advisable; but window banners and shop-window 'come-ons' are imperative.

The entry form
Side 1

IDENTIFY THESE ASSISTANTS
AND WIN
A TROLLEYFUL OF GROCERIES

Enter this simple competition – now – and win a trolleyful of groceries of your choice.

All you have to do is identify the six assistants whose silhouettes appear overleaf. Each of our assistants is wearing a name-tag – so it's easy.

Once you've identified them, write their names beneath the appropriate silhouette. Fill in your name and address. Then drop this entry form into the 'Silhouettes Competition' box at the check-out.

The first correct entry drawn on Wednesday XXst May will be the winner.

The winner will be notified within 24 hours of the draw. Then we'll ask you to come back and fill one of our service trolleys with whatever goods you care to choose.

And you can take as long as you wish to fill it!

A TROLLEYFUL OF GROCERIES COULD
BE WORTH £70 – OR MORE.

Side 2

HERE'S YOUR CHANCE
TO WIN
A TROLLEYFUL OF GROCERIES

(See overleaf)

Here are the silhouettes of the six assistants you have to identify

(Six silhouettes with name-space beneath each)

Name ....
Address ....
....
Telephone no. ....

While you're here, take advantage of today's special offers on a wide range of groceries.

(Include, on either side, balloons or flashes containing special offer products and prices.)

(Name of shop)

Figure 15

Your press ad would follow the format and the copy gist of Side 1. If you can run to it, include the products and prices, too.

Window display

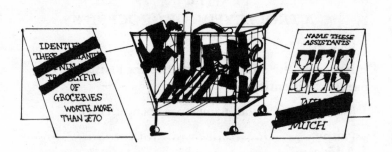

Figure 16

I think this is pretty self-explanatory.

You might consider inviting a local personality or dignitary to make the draw on your behalf, because there will be PR mileage in such a ploy.

Promo 4

Number plate pontoon

You have a showroom jammed with used cars, and these must be shifted in something of a hurry to make way for new models.

Run a press ad for three consecutive days before the event, to the effect: '*Play number plate pontoon and save big money on a Bloggs used car.*'

In the ad, you publish a list of 'hands' based on the registration numbers of the used vehicles concerned. Thus, any plate number adding up to 21 will receive a massive discount on the published price. Similarly, plate totals of 20, 19, 18, 17 and 16 will come in for progressively lesser discounts.

Clearly, customers have to visit the showroom to 'play' – which is when you work your charm on them.

A broader, and perhaps more 'entertaining' way to implement this idea, is to base the promotion on a single numeral: say on 7s. Thus, if a plate contains one 7, the discount on the published price of the car is £50. Two 7s, and you agree to give £100 off the price. Three 7s – the top 'hand' – and you allow £150 off.

Since you are aware of the registration numbers of your stock, you can organize the promotion around any single numeral, or any permutation, group or series of numerals, you so choose. You engineer it so that whatever discounts may be given, the original offer price covers them adequately enough for you to make at least a small profit.

Promo 5

Play detective

This one can be implemented by industrial or commercial enterprises wishing to push regular supplies of material and to put order forms into the hands of buyers.

Based on the ubiquitous *Cluedo* board-game, the promotion allows entrants to play detective over a series of mailings.

Here's how it works:

An initial, two-colour (A3 folded) mailer, outlining a classic, country house murder-mystery scenario, is sent to nominated buyers. You know the sort of thing I mean: Major Ayes-Watter is found dead in the library – stabbed neatly through the heart with an oriental dagger. This is accompanied, wouldn't you know it, by an order form for supplies of whatever it is you are selling. Thus, you make it clear that if the buyer doesn't place an order, he can't enter the competition.

So, the first mailer sets the murder scene, and two or three subsequent mailings (printed black and white this time, and reduced to A5) issue additional clues as to the identity of who dunnit. You shouldn't need more than four suspects: Fifi, the French maid; Lord Luvvus; Canon Fodder; and Mrs Buyer-Mile. To bring the characters to life, commission simple line drawings of each and use them throughout the promotion.

What the competitor has to do is evaluate the clues and nominate the murderer. He does this in an appropriate space on the final mailing.

So here's what you've got.

Week one
Initial mailer setting the scene, identifying the victim, and developing the characters. (Your order form goes with this one.)

Week two
Acknowledgement of order – which has already been delivered. Additional characterizations and storyline.

Week three.
Invoice. Clues and red-herrings to the identity of the killer.

Week four
Order form. Final clues. The buyer submits his solution to the killing. With luck, he also gives you another order.

The correct identity of the murderer, with supporting

evidence, should be lodged with your solicitor. Suitably sealed, of course. Prizes for correct solutions could be anything you'd care to offer. But might I suggest you invite the winners to one of those 'Murder Weekends', which are organized via many hotels in the UK, and which involve the guests in a 'real-life' murder mystery? They're not expensive; and they are great fun. And you'll be able to get close to your customer. Your local theatre ticket agency or travel service will give you the details.

Anyway, you don't by any means have to adhere to the sequence or timescale given above. Just one mailer could be made to do the entire job. Or, indeed, you might find it more beneficial to request a firm order in return for every additional set of clues. I've left it all deliberately loose in order to foster wider interpretation.

But I can see this idea working well where you need to wean buyers away from competitors; and where you require those buyers to give you repeat orders for your stationery, floppy-disks, bedding plants, sand and gravel, or what-have-you.

The promotion need not cost the earth – about £3,000 should take care of a 500-strong mailing list, and the prizes, quite adequately. And if that's all you have to lay out as a promotional/advertising spend for the year, it will be a job well done at nominal expenditure. (Should you need to restrict the number of winners, incorporate a tie-breaker.) Even as I think about it, I'm sure that a simplified version could be launched for a third of that amount.

In any event, the scheme has a lot of mileage; and you should get a big kick out of devising the murder mystery. To tell you the truth, I can't wait to do it.

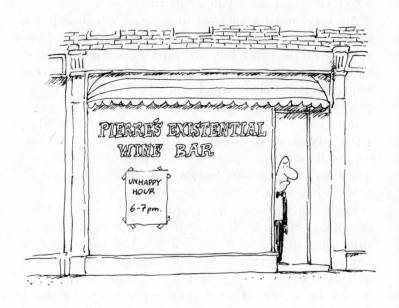

10   A few for the road

This chapter provides a diverse selection of ads, mailers and promotional material which may, with a little imagination, be adjusted and drafted into working for a variety of businesses. I've made the explanations of them deliberately brief so as not to inhibit adaptation.

1   A Cinderella for traffic

**IF THE SHOES FIT,
YOU WIN THE SHOES.**

**IF THEY'RE TOO TIGHT,
YOU WIN THE TIGHTS.**

Figure 17

A window display – complete with a pair of spotlit shoes – and an ad if you can afford it. The size of the shoes is *unspecified*.

If the right Cinderella comes along, and the shoes fit, she wins the shoes. However, a pair of tights is given to all those who fail.

2 Cut-price drink ad

PRICES SLOSHED!

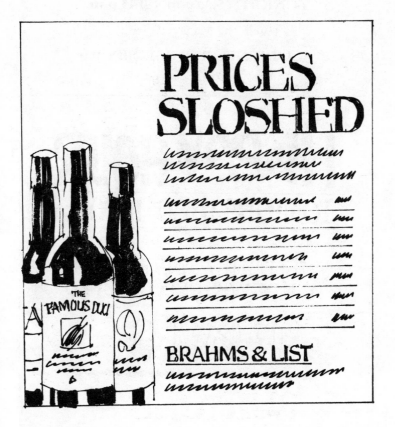

Figure 18

A straight ad detailing the price cuts, or a window display. Could also be used in conjunction with the following as a point-of-sale back-up to pub happy hours or silly half-hours.

3   Pub traffic

HAPPY HOUR
TONIGHT: 5.30 p.m. till 11 p.m.

(Well, the Manager's Irish)

ALL DRINKS REDUCED BY 10p

Figure 19

An ad or point-of-sale.

4   Diamond promotion

**OPENING TOMORROW
THE ONLY
SUPERMARKET
THAT OFFERS YOU
CARATS**

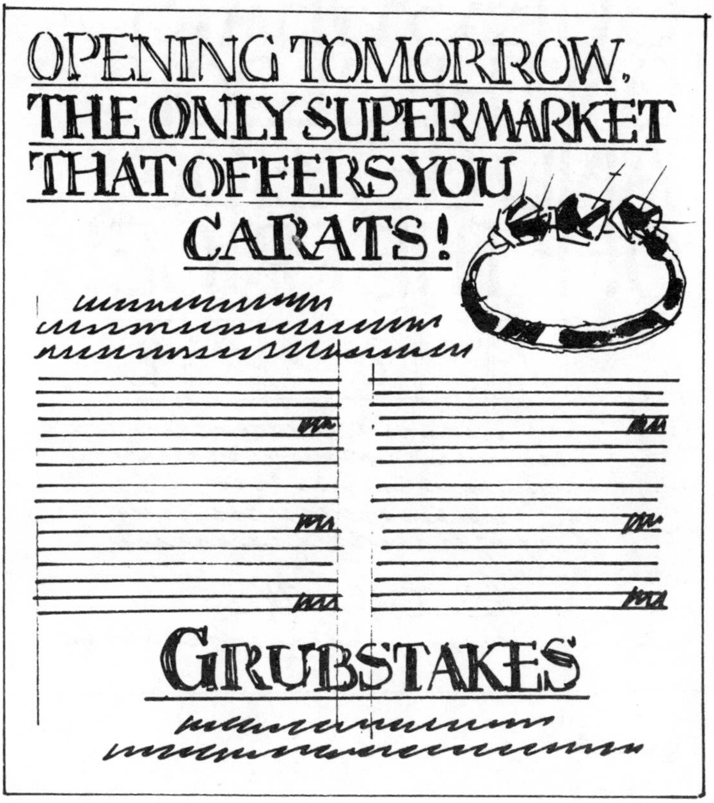

Figure 20

The ad launch of a new supermarket (video centre, clothes shop, whatever). Organize a simple competition around certain of your product prices – which have to be identified. Then draw the entries and give away a 9–carat ring or other jewellery.

5   Garage traffic

**GUESS WHAT'S ON THE CLOCK
AND GET £100 OFF
THE PRICE**

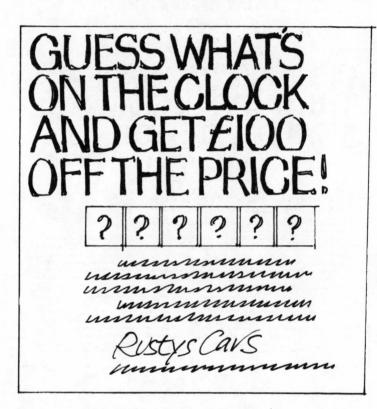

Figure 21

This ad launches a used car promotion. Publish a list of all the cars in the sale – along with year of manufacturer and, if you like the *average* yearly mileage of each vehicle. Then announce that if the punter can guess, within 500 miles each way, the mileage of the car he fancies, you'll give him a £100 (substantial?) price reduction. (Your salespeople will obviously use their discretion with regard to near-miss guesses.)

6 Department store sale

**A THREE-PIECE
GARDEN KIT FOR A
THRU'PENNY BIT**

Figure 22

An ad announcing a sale in which everyone who tenders an old threepenny piece will receive the garden kit (gloves, hand-fork, hand-spray?). *While stocks last*, of course.

The ad would also detail your major sale bargains.

Or, for a summer sale, for which you are stuck for a theme, how about:

**THE
NOT-THE-JANUARY-SALE
SALE!**

7   A promotion for any store

**SPEND £5 IN
OUR PLACE
AND YOU COULD SPEND
A WEEKEND
IN HIS PLACE**

Figure 23

It costs very little to send someone to Paris for a weekend.
This could be the prize for a simple in-store competition.

But since there must be proof of purchase – the fiver – use
the tie-breaker.

8   In-store competition

HIDDEN TREASURE

The concept of a desert island with a hidden treasure as a promotional gambit is not a new one. I'll go even farther and say that the ploy of hiding a valuable object and asking punters to find it is as old as village fêtes.

However, on every occasion that I've operated the hidden pirate's treasure device, it has proved to be a crowd-pleasure, a response-puller, and an all-round winner.

The real beauty of the hidden treasure routine is that it can be run in a variety of ways:

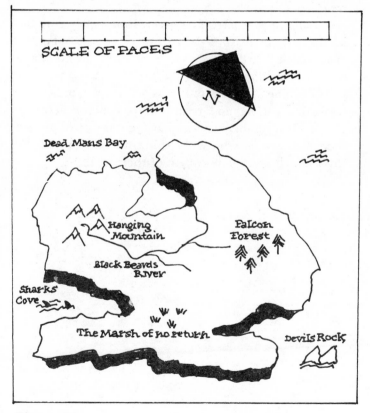

Figure 24

1   *On a genuine beach.* You simply divide the area of sand into a series of equal size plots and key each plot. In one way or another, the participants 'win' a plot and dig it to find the treasure.

In this case, obviously, the treasure is nothing more than a small box which contains a card naming the prize.

Operated thus, the scheme provides a magnificent opportunity to pull customers out of their offices and get them face-to-face with your sales staff. (Remember to ask permission from the local authority before digging commences.)

2   *As an in-store model.* Build a polystyrene model of a desert island and, via a simple elimination competition, ask the winners to place pins wherever they think the treasure is located.

3   *As a competition mailer.* You give various clues as to the location of the treasure – 20 paces west of Falcon Forest, cross Black Beard's River, etc. – either in one go or as a series of mailings.

The winners then draw a cross on the map, indicating treasure location, and return it to you for judging. You'd be agreeably surprised at the number of grown men and women who will spend time on a puzzle like this. Usually to the detriment of their work.

9   Discount jeweller

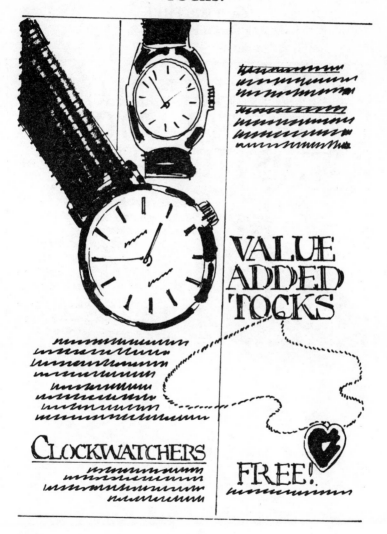

Figure 25

Straight ad – straight offer. A free 9 carat locket and chain
(or other desirable gift) with every watch.

10   Record store

**YOU'LL JUST LOVE
THE SOUND
OF THIS FREE
OFFER**

Figure 26

Again, a straight incentive offer: a free cassette with every two cassettes/or LPs bought. Could easily be adapted for shops retailing domestic sound systems, or in-car stereo cassette units.

11   Clothing store sale

CLOTHING DOWN SALE!

Figure 27
Speaks for itself – doesn't it?

12   Auto-parts centre

IF WE DON'T STOCK IT
SCRAP THE CAR

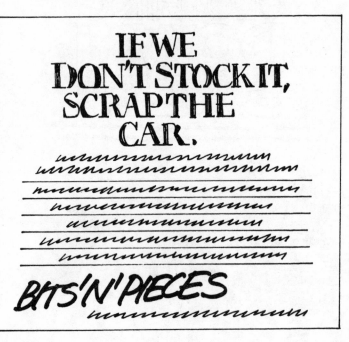

Figure 28

An unsophisticated exercise which makes the implied promise that Bits'n'Pieces very probably stocks parts for every make of car on the road. Implicit, too, is the offer of those parts to the reader. This ad could be run in just about any publication, in any size. Would do a proper job in *Yellow Pages*, too.

13 Pub promotion

If you ever need an up-market competition – one which requires more thought than the average quiz – try this.

PUB NAMES

You ask competitors to think of a town and then invent a pub name appropriate to it.

For instance, there could be the Centipede at Crawley, the Highwayman at Andover, the Whole Loaf at Nuneaton, not to mention the Four Flusher at Deal.

This game is as addictive as salted peanuts. You'll receive entries like the Two Cubes at Dyce, the Disco at Rockingham, the Milkmaid at Huddersfield, and the Small Man at Littlehampton, not to mention many that will be quite unprintable.

This one, however, will only work with a fairly literate audience. But it will work.

14 Used car promotion

CAR KEY PUZZLER

Here's a nice one for filling showrooms with people.

1 Start by publishing an ad in the local paper for three or four consecutive days. The ad contains a large illustration of a car key. (The number is obscured.)

   You announce that this key fits a particular car (new or used) and the car can be won.

2 The car is also featured in the press, and is given the five-star 'dressing-up' treatment in your showroom.

3 We ask readers to cut out the key picture and bring it along to the showroom during a specified period. On that day, you will display a peg-board holding the keys of every used vehicle in the showroom. (For convenience, these could be photographs blown up, or

larger than life cardboard cut-outs.) The punter is request to compare the picture with the display of keys; and he selects the key which, in his opinion, is the one in the picture.

4   Your salesman then escorts him to the 'prize' car to try the key. If it fits, he wins it. If it doesn't, the salesman steers him towards the one it does fit (your man will obviously have a list showing what fits what). He then offers him an unrefusable deal.

5   During the initial key-choosing exercise, *no keys are taken off the board*. Numbered duplicates are used when the customer makes his selection. This avoids a correct choice being made, in a crowded showroom, by simple elimination.

Car key ad

THIS KEY DRIVES AWAY
THIS CAR – FREE!

Find the real key at our Bash Street
showroom and the car is yours

(Picture of key – number obscured)	(Picture of car) **Prize car – worth £1800!**

Bring this key picture to our Bash Street showroom within the next X days. And you could drive away in our prize car.

An immaculate, 1983 Falcon.

All you have to do is match the picture with a bank of keys. Pick the one that starts the Falcon – and it's yours.

No strings. Nothing to pay.

Of course, only one person can win. But if you're not lucky, we'll give you the consolation of a first-class deal on any of our range of completely overhauled used cars.

And we mean a first-class deal. In fact, we *know* you won't find a better buy anywhere.

So drop in soon with the picture. You could drive out with that Falcon.

(Company name and address)

15 Ad for the small builder

A small-scale builder, with not much money to chuck around on advertising, could use the following both as a headline and a tag-line. The latter would sit comfortably on all of his letterheads, compliments slips and literature generally. It's a basic line which sums up his range of services. Note how the company name is used as a kind of builder's mark. (We'd better give the company a name: Briggs & Mortar.)

**BRIGGS & MORTAR
THE UNMISTAKABLE MARK
OF A MASTER BUILDER**

Figure 29

16   Ad for musical instrument shop

How to advertise the widest range of instruments in the
smallest possible space. Like this, maybe:

**LARGO'S. THE ROCK, FOLK
JAZZ, PUNK, CONCERT
SHOP**

Figure 30

With copy:
**Whether you're new on the music scene, or an
all-singing, all-strumming, all-drumming professional, you'll find everything you need at
Largo's.**

And at the right price, too.

**Drums. Guitars. Trombones. Oboes. Key-
boards. Vibes. (etc.)**

With amplifiers and accessories to match.

More kit, in fact, than you could wave a baton at.

What's more. We like you to try before you buy.

Which means some days we have a great jam going . . . right in the shop.

Why not drop in and wing something – like soon?

(Company name and address)

Should this same music shop require to make a push on individual instruments, in this case guitars, here's one way of doing so:

ALL YOU NEED TO PLAY
A LARGO GUITAR
IS A LARGO GUITAR

Spanish guitars from only £XX.XX. Electric from only £XX.XX.

Westone. Marlin. Hondo. Kay. Arion and Encore.

Plus a complete range of amplifiers and easy-play tutors.

Drop in soon and try one for size. In fact, try the lot . . . it's the only way to choose.

(Company name and address)

The ad can be adapted for any instrument you chose, though with suitable come-on lines. i.e. for keyboards: 'Drop in soon and try a few runs'. Or, for drums: 'Drop in soon and get behind a kit'. And so on.

17 Office equipment poster campaign

An office equipment firm, which retails business systems – dictating systems, Fax machines, and the like – wants to locate secretaries and office managers with a cheap poster campaign. This could run on tube cards, or bus interiors.

The firm is known as Quintet Business Systems.

VISIONS OF THE
PERFECT OFFICE SYSTEM
No. 1

● **Two-hour coffee breaks.**
● **Four secretaries to each executive.**
● **An Electron Dictating System.**

Issued as a public service by
Quintet Business Systems
(Address/Phone)

You can't beat the system

VISIONS OF THE
PERFECT OFFICE SYSTEM
No 2

● **Single red rose, per secretary, per day.**
● **Fridays off for shopping.**
● **An Adivetti Screenprinter.**

Issued as a public service by
Quintet Business Systems

You can't beat the system

Or, for a larger poster:

QBS NEWS BULLETIN
Stop Press

● **The pound has fallen three points against the Matabele gumbo bean.**
● **End of the world predicted for 3.15 p.m. Wednesday. (Or, failing that, Thursday.)**
● **Ms Samantha Goodbody, of 3 The Mews,**

Clapham Broadway, talks boss into buying
an Electron Dictating System.

Quintet Business Systems (etc.)

18   Antique/bric-a-brac/crafts shop

Possibly the cheapest way to get read is via the lineage ads in
the Sales and Wanted columns of your local paper. In which
case, a series of 'personals' usually goes down well.

> **ARTFUL.** I adore you. Picked up a marvellous period
> fireplace at Magpie Antique and Craft Galleries.
> Thanks: ADAM.

> **BRIC-A-BRAC.** Will meet you Friday for a rum-
> mage round at Magpie Antique and Craft Galleries.
> KNICK-KNACK.

> **DIAMOND JIM.** Give me a ring. I've waited an
> eternity for another engagement at Magpie Antique
> and Craft Galleries. Love: AMETHYST.

> **CLOCKWATCHER.** Must see your face soon.
> Can't wait to get my hands on you at Magpie Antique
> and Craft Galleries. MAINSPRING.

Although I have my fingers crossed and the garlic ready
to hand, I would like to imagine that whatever business you
happen to be in, the foregoing will give you some
eminently useable ideas and easily adaptable concepts. The
examples are by no means exhaustive; so I wouldn't claim
for a moment that we've covered every single eventuality.
Further, none of the examples is in any way a work of art.
But what I do know, in my heart if nowhere else, is that if
their sentiments are followed somewhat closely, you won't
go very far wrong.

11   Fight the good fight

If advertising is about anything, it is about competition. And to compete is to fight. Someone once said that the best method of defence is to attack. That's undeniable. So the low-budget advertiser *must* believe in advertising that doesn't pussyfoot, that pulls no punches, that minces no words, and doesn't go halfway round the world to make its point.

However, don't take me up wrongly. In your promotional activities, you shouldn't aim to go about upsetting people.

Except, of course, your competitors.

There now follows a partly proleptical broadcast on behalf of the low-budget party. In fact, eight well-chosen precepts that will help put some wallop into your work.

1   Much of today's advertising is completely ordinary. It risks little, therefore it gains little. When formulating advertising, it is your job to do more than just publish facts about yourself and your product. Your function is to motivate consumers; to challenge long-held beliefs; to confirm choices; and to change attitudes.

2   The only way to devise effective advertising is by first formulating a precise marketing brief. Don't lift a pen, nor ink a brush, until the brief is right.

What are you going to say? *How* are you going to say it? To *whom* are you going to say it? And *where* are you going to say it?

Get these answers right and, suddenly, the campaign is in top gear and gaining momentum. Get them wrong and it will never be out of bottom.

This isn't merely a piece of patronizing couéism. It's a real, proven, indisputable, copper-bottomed fact.

3   Keeping up with the Jones's is a terrible thing. Lagging behind them is even worse. Many advertisers spending five, ten, or twenty thousand pounds develop a complex when they consider other advertisers spending three or four hundred thousand.

The get envious, and they get worried. They think their money can't possibly buy them the same standard of work and the same standard of service.

They are wrong. As I hope I've already indicated; and as I am sure you will prove for yourself.

4   Did you know that in binary arithmetic 1 + 1 doesn't equal 2? With every respect to higher mathematicians everywhere, if you can believe that you can believe anything.

However, there is one field in which you would be wise to follow the binary line quite closely. And that's in the selection of your media. The lowest rate, plus the highest circulation doesn't always equal the best buy.

Not by a long chalk.

If people were numbers, preparing a media schedule would be deadly simple. All you'd need would be a slide rule, a set of log tables and a calculator. But they're not; and it isn't; and you don't.

You need something else as well. A secret ingredient worth more than ten guineas an ounce. You need nous; and you need good old gut-feeling.

The same gut-feeling which urged you to manufacture that Christmas-tree stand, or design that better mouse-trap, in the first place.

5   Sssh? Or hoop-la. Hard-sell or soft-sell – which is the most effective? The way to look at it is this.

It doesn't matter much whether you catch a trout with a fly or a tickle. Just so long as you catch it. And it doesn't matter whether you sell merchandise by shouting its values at people, or by sidling up and saying: 'Psst! Want to buy a . . .' Just so long as you sell it.

But remember this. There are an awful lot of trout more

susceptible to the tickle than to the fly. And an awful lot of ears deaf to shouts, but wide open to whispers.

6   Can advertising be all things to all men? Decidedly not!

If you have something worth saying, say it directly; or say it provocatively; or cleverly, cheekily, funnily, or stridently. But never, ever say it half-heartedly.

Of course, the more positive your advertising, the more probable it is that someone won't like it. But the more certain it is that many others will. And losses on swings have a habit of becoming highly profitable gains on roundabouts.

All rules, they say, have exceptions, but I can't think, offhand, of any exception to this: that advertising which sets out to please everyone is likely to end up by pleasing no one at all.

7   Advertising has developed a language of its own; full of superlatives and words which ordinary people don't ordinarily use. Nouns like 'boon'. Verbs like 'beautify'. Adjectives like 'fabulous', 'blissful' and 'stupendous'. Tired advertising words, all of them.

The fact is, when you conceive advertising – when you write copy and draw pictures – you should strive to be straight to the point without being dull. Without creating false excitement. And without obviously exaggerated overstatements.

In the first place, your audience will understand you a lot better. In the second place, they will believe you a lot more readily.

8   I don't quite know how to say this without drawing from you a huge sigh and an irritated heavenward glance. But are you absolutely sure there is a market for what you are selling? And if there is, do you know where it is located? And if you do, have you a carefully worked out plan for reaching it?

I just thought I'd ask.

★   ★   ★

I don't expect these pages to have made any great difference to your life. Nor can I picture you leaping around with an expression of divine inspiration on your face. All I can say if they have, and you are, then you are either leading a remarkably dull life or you have been at the cooking sherry.

It is my duty, in conclusion, to tell you that there is no such thing as the infallible ad. Anybody who tells you differently should be viewed with the same suspicion as the man who: (a) offers you the key to the door of the fourth dimension; (b) professes to have perfected perpetual motion; (c) knows how to square the circle; or (d) pours you a shot of the elixir of life.

I trust you take the point.

What I sincerely hope, above all, is that this book will work for you. If it does, and you change overnight from a low-budget advertiser to a high-budget advertiser, please don't go to all the trouble of leaving me something in your will. That would be altogether too generous. Far better, I think, to simply remember that it was me who put you on the right road . . . and send a modest cheque straight away.

You will – won't you?

Glossary of terms

Air-brush illustration An air-brush is a type of pen into which ink is loaded, and through which air is blown (by compressor or mouth). The resultant ink spray is played on to the surface to be painted. The air-brush technique is characterized by strong colours, intermingling of colours, and the heavily accentuated outlines of curved subjects.

Body copy The descriptive material in an advertisement. It represents your one and only opportunity to put your message across.

Budget The amount of money allocated for the advertising effort. (See Chapter 1 for a rule-of-thumb method of assessing a budget figure.)

Camera ready Any piece of artwork suitable for print reproduction. Camera ready, as determined by newspapers and periodicals, usually means the complete artwork for an advertisement, with all the ingredients pasted down. This artwork is photographed and a printing 'plate' made from the negative.

Campaign Your overall advertising effort for a particular product. (Any series of advertisements or commercials projecting a similar theme.)

Circulation The total print-run of a newspaper/magazine. (Not to be confused with *readership*.)

Concept testing The marketing discipline of assessing the 'desire to purchase' a given product. This is done by researching its viability with wholesalers and retailers – and by quizzing a cross-section of consumers taken from the socio-economic group at which the product will be aimed.

Copy testing A similar exercise to the above, but where specific body copy, headlines, tag-lines, and so on, are previewed by an invited audience. Audience reactions are noted and taken into account.

Corporate identity A company's individuality. Its unique way of doing things. (The company colours, letterhead design, logotype, namestyle, uniforms, vehicle livery – all working together to project a special identity.)

Cost-per-thousand readership The cost of the advertising space divided into the actual readership of a newspaper or magazine, and the 'per-thousand' rate calculated.

Demand philosophy In essence, an appraisal of what a given market requires from you – if anything. (If there *is* a market for Christmas-tree stands, say, does the market want those stands painted/unpainted? Packaged/unpackaged? Foldaway or rigid construction?)

Designer A commercial artist. Also called a visualizer or art director.

Direct Mail Any publicity material (brochures, leaflets, sales letters) sent direct to a potential customer. Also known as *mailers* and *mail shots*.

Drive-time Radio station parlance for the premium broadcasting period, i.e. when motorists are travelling to and from work. (Around 7 a.m. to 9 a.m., and 3 p.m. to 6 p.m.)

Ear spaces Those tiny advertising spaces located on either side of a newspaper's masthead (title). Frequently called title corners or ear pieces.

Finished art The final mechanical, pasted-up layout of type and picture. Artwork ready for the camera. (See *camera ready*.)

Half-tone illustration A photograph in print. The process involves placing a 'screen' over the photograph, with a result that the photograph is broken down into dots. The screens are made with a varying number of screen-dot lines to the millimetre – depending on application. For newspapers the range is, roughly, 50 to 85, and for magazines 120 to 150 lines per 25 mm.

Hard sell Hard-hitting advertising that pulls no verbal or visual punches. (The antithesis of *soft sell*.)

Headline The major element in a press advertisement, designed to summarize, give essential information about, or interest readers in the bones of the ad. (More properly, it's a platform from which to make an offer or give a promise about the product.)

Incentives Promotional give-aways (anything from keyrings to exotic holidays) to encourage the buying of a product, or to encourage employees to put up a better sales performance.

ITCA/AIRC The watchdog organization which monitors all radio and television advertising.

Jingle Any piece of music, orchestral or vocal, written specifically for use as a constituent part of a commercial.

Knock-and-drop Leaflets or literature distributed door to door by hand.

Layout A rough design, visual, or scamp, of what an advertisement will look like when it appears in the papers.

Level The optimum volume, in decibels, of a radio recording. Recording engineers set their equipment to zero DBS and record a 'line-up' tone at the beginning of each tape. Thus, the radio station regulates its equipment to zero on the tone so that the recording is broadcast at a standard level.

Library music Stock recordings held by studios and radio stations and which are produced especially for commercial use.

Line drawings A pen-and-ink, black-and-white drawing that has no tones to speak of. Even so, the line drawing can be quite detailed and is especially useful for 'artist's' impressions of houses not yet built, or for creating purely imaginary illustrations.

Logotype A symbol or graphic device (often a word or series of letters) closely associated with a product, manufacturer or service and by which they may be readily indentified.

Marketing The art of defining a market for a product, or vice versa.

Master tape   A tape – usually 2 in – on to which each of the various tracks of a radio commercial are recorded. Thus, each of the elements of voice, music and sound effect may either be deleted, re-mixed, or reconstituted for future use.

Media   Loosely, any platform from which to launch an advertising campaign: press, radio, TV, direct mail – even bus sides.

Media schedule   A record or timetable of the newspapers, and magazines, in which your advertising will appear.

Opportunities to see (OTS)   The number of times your advertising may be seen by the readership of a given publication. The OTS figure is determined by multiplying the readership by the number of times your ad will appear.

Point-of-sale   Any item of publicity (posters, counter displays, shelf-wobblers, etcetera) displayed at the position where a purchase is to be made.

Press release   A letter or item of written material about a product or service distributed to newspapers and periodicals and which is intended for publication.

Product development   The process of assessing the manufacturing quality that the target market demands.

Production   An all-embracing term for any 'mechanical' work (typesetting, photography, plate-making) undertaken to produce ads or printed material.

Promotion   A term which may be applied to a single competition or incentive, or to the entire mix of advertising for a given product.

Proofreading   The responsibility for checking 'proofs' – the trial impressions of any piece of printwork – lies with the customer. In which case, check them thoroughly.

Proofreading correction marks   When correcting proofs, the reader makes two separate marks or instructions on the proof itself: one in the body of the text, and one in the margin. Anyone required to read their own proofs – and you should never leave this job to someone else – would be wise to pick up the definitive work on the subject: a small but informative volume titled: *Hart's Rules For Compositors and Readers* (Oxford University Press).

Public relations The purpose of PR is to create an auspicious atmosphere around your business so that trading may be carried out in a climate of goodwill. This is achieved by releasing news about the company to the public at large by way of the various media.

Rate card The tariff of costs, space-sizes and positions offered by the press media; and the list of charges per time-segment given out by radio and TV stations.

Readership The total number of readers of a newspaper or magazine; always bearing in mind that a paper may be read by more people than just the purchaser.

Readership profile A breakdown of the socio-economic groupings, occupations, interests, etc., of a newspaper or magazine.

Reel-to-reel Otherwise the ¼ in recording tape required by radio stations for transmission purposes.

Run-of-paper Meaning that the advertiser buys no special position for his advertisement. It will therefore appear wherever the paper's make-up people care to put it.

Socio-economic breakdown The six established degrees of social background and income level from which to determine your market; and at which to pitch your advertising effort.

Soft sell Advertising that is characterized by its gentle, persuasive stance – as opposed to a hard-selling, bombastic line.

Solus Any piece of press advertising which sits alone on a page amidst editorial.

Tag-Line Or strap line. A line of copy, usually sitting close to the logo, and which sums up the quality of the product or establishes the philosophy of the company, e.g. *'The best tools you can lay hands on.'*

USP Unique selling proposition. The major selling point of a product or service. Works faster; digs deeper; takes up less space, etc. The selling point which establishes it as being superior to any similar product.

Index